Numerology

Maximize Your Life, Discover Opportunities and Decode Your Destiny

Kevin Jobson

or indirect, that are incurred as a result of the use of the information contained within this document, including, but not limited to, errors, omissions, or inaccuracies.

Table of Contents

Introduction

Did you know that our ancient ancestors used complex math to build places of power? They used this math to build megaliths and pyramids that modern people can no longer explain.

It may seem entirely impossible to us, but somehow, our ancestors were able to use complex mathematical concepts to build structures that baffle us today. We have theories about how monuments like the pyramids were built but no real, hard evidence. Nor do we know why these monuments were built. The henges and pyramids we see are sites of obvious significance, but many of these sites were built for reasons we have no record of.

What we do know is that our ancestors built many of these sites with the stars and constellations themselves in mind. It is believed that they did this by understanding numbers in a way we have lost. The reason they used this math is that they believed the vibrations and energy of the sites could be manipulated by the math used to construct these places.

These buildings were made this way to tune into the frequencies of energy in the world and the greater universe around us. It was a way of channeling the energy into the visitors of these sites to help them feel more in tune with the universe.

But this connection to the universe is hardly a thing of the past. Even today, we know that our star signs and the seasons of our year carry messages, and we accept this kind of thinking as something inherently human.

Hello, dear reader, and welcome to the world of numerology. It's a world that looks to unveil these secrets in our modern world, both in the physical and metaphysical sense.

If you have come to this journey with no knowledge of numerology and are looking to learn, or if you already have a basic understanding of the concepts and simply want to expand your horizons, I welcome you and thank you for joining me on this journey that we are about to embark on.

You may be feeling skeptical of what I have to tell you. Often, when someone introduces an idea to a conversation that feels different somehow, it's as if our minds cannot accept this new way of thinking. This idea may even seem alien to us. Don't be alarmed. This kind of skepticism is healthy; however, on this journey, we will come to see that this skepticism is unwarranted.

We live in a world where we can begin to divine a purpose for ourselves and see the patterns in our lives. We can see our strengths and weaknesses and how these affect each of our relationships, both human and ethereal.

It's a world where our souls and the things they yearn for can be seen, deciphered, discussed, and understood. It's a place where the relationships between our energies are the key to happiness and where the relationships throughout our being can be balanced, decluttered, and allowed to thrive.

We can start to understand why we may be feeling out of sorts, depressed, less like ourselves, or even suddenly euphoric. How?

Simple. All of this can be explained by the numbers that govern us. This is numerology.

But what is numerology? What real-world lessons can we draw from its seemingly spiritual principles? And what lessons can we apply to our lives? Is it all-powerful and all-meaningful?

Regardless of if you are a skeptic or believer, I wholeheartedly believe that this journey is one worth traveling, that this is a road that cannot be ignored because of how integral to us all numbers truly are.

In this journey, we will discuss numerology and how, through the principles we learn, it can help us to better define ourselves, our relationships, and how we plan and develop projects.

We will also look at some of the different schools of thought in numerology and discuss the parallels between numerology and religion. We will look at everything from base numbers to how different people's vibrations can affect us. We will even cover how we can begin to declutter our minds and lives.

Throughout our journey together, we will consider the spiritual and practical power of numbers and begin to understand that what we feel and how we act are linked to those same numbers.

Everything from our date of birth to our very name is governed by numbers. This power extends to how our soul explores the ethereal world, which planets affect us, which numbers benefit us and which don't, as well as which personalities complement each other. Knowledge of these numbers can improve your life, and I will offer some advice in regard to the various numbers and what to do when your planet is ascending and in retrograde.

All this information is discussed so that when our time on this journey together comes to an end, you can start to use your newfound knowledge and energy to better maximize yourself and those around you.

You will be able to better capitalize on and see opportunities in front of you. You will understand who you are on a deeper, more spiritual level. You will look at not just yourself but all the reasons and motivations we have in our souls and futures.

So, come with me, dear reader. Let us learn things that will surprise us about ourselves and our world. We will uncover truths we always suspected but never could prove and discover the part of us that has lain dormant. This will all be revealed by the numbers and vibrations of our very souls, which we will embrace to better capture our true, full self.

Let us dive into the depths of all of the numbers that define our lives, that guide us in more ways than we realize or thought possible and in more places than we imagined. In the end, we will begin to see parts of our souls that we may have neglected previously.

Let us set sail on the energies we can nurture and learn to be our best and most complete self. Welcome on board. Thank you for joining this journey.

Chapter 1:

Understanding Numbers

Here, we stand together at the start of our journey, dear reader, a journey where we will aim to unlock the foundations of our destiny and the universe to understand the grand plan of the cosmos itself.

This is a journey where we can self-analyze and also start to help those around us by adjusting our vibrations, planning ahead, and applying what we learn to the greatest effect. Of course, all journeys start with a single step. In our case, we have a few complex questions to ask.

Firstly, what is numerology? Where does it come from? What variations of numerology are there? How does numerology apply to us?

This is where our journey together truly begins, with a simple set of questions, because to apply numerology, we must consider its origins. We must begin to try and understand it.

These questions do not intend to undermine. Instead, the goal is to encourage and understand so that we can begin to see and unpack the inner workings of numerology. We need to start to disarm our guarded, skeptical self. This is a part of us that is important for us to embrace as it is the source of our difficult questions.

Once we have an understanding of what numerology is, we can start to ask ourselves those bigger questions from our skeptical mind, allowing us to tackle much grander ideas and understand ourselves on a much deeper level.

We can start to unpack the universe itself, understanding our souls and our destiny in a way that we may otherwise never get to see. This is a journey that will feature many complex ideas, and we will tackle them together.

And once we arrive at our journey's end, we can look back at the question "what is numerology?" through changed eyes and see that the world is far bigger than we first could see.

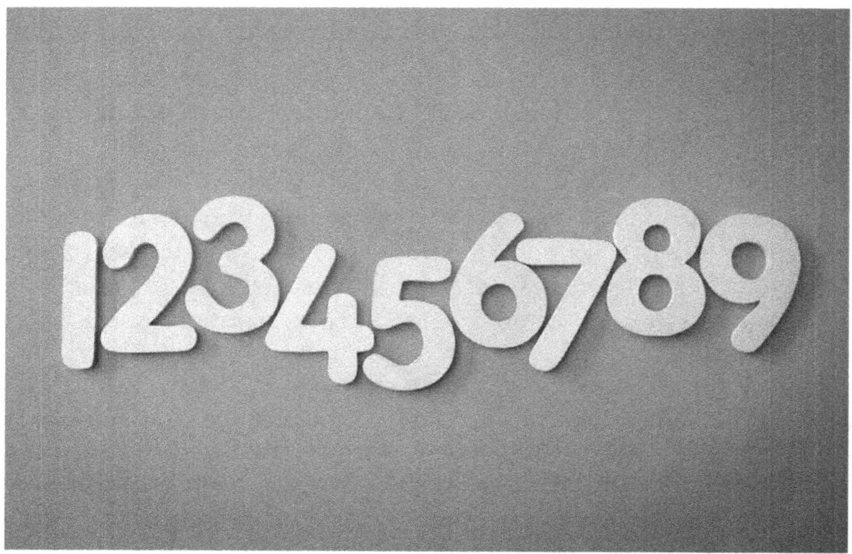

What Is Numerology?

Numerology is a complex, spiritual belief in the power of numbers. It is a belief that these numbers affect everything in our lives, from our relationships to our business deals, from our homes to our souls. Numbers are found everywhere and touch everything in both places you may realize and in those you have not considered.

Numerology is also the belief that our energy and our vibrations both affect and are affected by the energies around us and the energies that come from the cosmos, the planets, and the very days and weeks we experience.

It is the understanding that the universe is far bigger than what we see and that our power to understand it is much greater than we have realized. It is the understanding that as much as we affect the world around us in our day-to-day lives, the days and years vibrate in a way we must come to understand, a way that is beneficial to us and those around us.

Numerology links to other cosmic disciplines, such as astrology, and allows us to look into our future and our destiny and see what they might hold for us.

It is of no surprise, then, that we also track these other disciplines through the lens of numbers, with our star signs falling into categories based on numbers, the influence those numbers have on us, and how the planets themselves affect those same vibrations.

Numerology is in everything, even in places you might not think. Did you know, for example, that all music is written with numbers in mind? Beats per bar, beats per minute, even the length and structure of any given song are thought of in numbers, with some musicians even writing their music to specific rhythms to appeal to the mind.

It is music where many believe that modern numerology began, with Pythagoras, the famous Greek mathematician, developing the idea of a relationship between music and numbers, a relationship that most music majors will tell you is real.

The same is also true in the everyday. Things like the pricing of a product and how much you weigh are presented to you with numbers, and these things all carry immense power. Numbers are everywhere, but not all numerologists look at numbers the same, which is perhaps where some of the skepticism comes from.

We will look first at how the thinking of numbers varies by looking at a couple of different schools of thought, how they are applied through science, and the relationship between numbers and astrology. This will give us an understanding of some of the core principles of the discipline. Then, we can start to look at the self and begin to explore our fates.

Numbers, you see, have been an important part of our society for centuries, with our ancestors building henges and temples, churches and monoliths, all from the principles of numbers and their divine links.

The Numbers We Already Use

Before we begin, we need to discuss the numbers we use in our everyday world and how they affect our lives. First and foremost, we have our age or the measurement of how long it has been since we were born. Unfortunately, many sections of society judge people purely on their age, leading to some shame around this number, particularly if it is higher. The use of age as a number, though, shows us how common an idea it is to apply an idea or identity to a number.

Next, we have buses, trains, and planes, which all use numbers to help differentiate their routes, times, destinations, and drivers so that you can identify the path each mode of transportation is going to take you.

Thirdly, we all have phone numbers. The gauge for many potentially romantic interactions is whether or not the parties want to exchange their real phone numbers, which is an expression of individual boundaries.

Our banks also use a lot of numbers. We have our PINs and account numbers. These numbers represent safety, control, and even power and wealth. When picking a PIN, for example, we pick a number that feels safe to us or has some special connotation to us. It may be a birthday or our parents' address. Even a number picked seemingly at random stems for our need to have a strong PIN.

By using these common numbers, we can see that we as a society already identify people by numbers. We already plan our path with numbers. We use numbers to determine our relationships and take safety and power from numbers.

As foreign as this concept may be, all of these are ideas we will look at in numerology. They are all core elements that we can draw from the numbers we will discuss and the things we already do.

The Different Schools of Thinking

When people discuss numerology, they are generally using it as an all-encompassing term for the broadest sense of the belief with the idea that all numerology is the same. While this is broadly accurate, you may be surprised to learn that there are multiple schools of thinking when it comes to numerology.

Many skeptics will say that the variances in the discipline can only prove the belief wrong, and while a healthy dose of skepticism is definitely helpful, the simple truth is that just because there are some different points of opinion does not make something false.

Yes, some elements of the various schools of discipline are different, but the truth is that more things are similar.

There are also parts of the world that we wouldn't consider to be influenced by the power of numbers or the belief in numerology. However, looking at them shows that even without this belief, there is a deeper connection to numbers within the human soul.

One of the core things to remember is that just because there are some disagreements on a topic doesn't make it any less powerful in our lives. Religious beliefs, for example, are sacred to us, and there is always plenty of debate there.

Additionally, many scientific theories have ongoing debates. Despite this, we still view those beliefs as true. Even if we don't fully understand the truth behind them, we know they are true. Numerology can be viewed in the same light.

The Pythagorean System

This is the system we initially touched on when we started this part of our journey. As mentioned earlier, Pythagoras was a Greek philosopher and mathematician. He not only came up with the theory of musical notes having a relationship with numbers, but he also realized that the vibrations of musical notes could be mathematically explained.

Oft credited as the father of Western numerology, Pythagoras used a method of adding the numerical values attributed to each letter. Then, he added the values of each number together to construct a value. Each number of that value was then added together to get a final number.

As an example, if the letters in your name were added together and came to 32 based on their assigned value, and the value of your surname was 48, you would then add 32 and 48 together, making 80. You would then add the 8 and the 0 together to get a final value of 8.

This end number is referred to as a digit sum. You'll see this term a lot throughout our journey. It is one of the most important numbers we will see.

The Chaldean System

While Pythagoras, who was born in 549 BC and died around 470 BC, is often credited as being the father of numerology, he was by no means the first to realize the cosmic connection between numbers and us as spiritual entities.

Sometimes referred to as the Babylonian numerology system, the Chaldean system dates back to around 625 BC and 539 BC. This system will, at first glance, appear incredibly similar to the Pythagorean system; however, the two have notable differences.

While both use a similar methodology, there are differences in how the digit sum for names is reached. For example, the Pythagorean system uses the base numbers of 1 through 9 as its basis for these sums, whereas the Chaldean system assigns each letter a value between 1 and 8, with 9 being a separate number that is used in other aspects of the belief but not in the calculations regarding names.

It is believed that this is due to the sacred nature of the number 9. The Chaldean system will be the one from which our journey through this book draws much of its lessons since it is the one I feel the deepest connection to and the one I feel best explains our world.

But numerology isn't restricted to schools of thought stemming from the past. We can also find evidence of numerology in science.

Science

When used in a scientific way, numerology is the study of patterns. The most famous one is Dirac's Large Numbers Hypothesis (LNH). A scientist named Paul Dirac made observations in 1937 that there were a large number of cosmic forces, for example, gravity, the proportion of the universe, and even mass, that shared mathematical constants.

What is interesting is that numerology shares this argument. It states that our energy and vibrations affect not only the people around us but also the universe and that we can look at and learn from this energy by using math.

The LNH looked at numbers that seemed to be coincidences and used equations to show a pattern, which is exactly what numerology is.

Another scientific belief based in numbers and math that applies to almost every human being walking the earth today is called binary.

Binary is a numeric system that uses 0 and 1 to represent information in a pattern of seemingly random 0s and 1s. It is the system from which all computing begins. These patterns power every device and every process on every device using the simple power of numbers to process complex and meaningful information.

Binary is believed to have originated as we know it now in the 16th century; however, there is evidence that ancient Egyptians and Chinese cultures used systems similar to binary, showing that our ancestors already knew how powerful and important numbers are.

Numbers are so powerful that even at a complex level, they, above all else, govern science, so we can begin to use these numbers to power and better ourselves and our outcomes.

Science even shows us that many of the world's great ancient sites seem to incorporate elements pertaining to math, numbers, and geometry to draw power into these sacred places. Places like Stonehenge or the Great Pyramids all use angles and complex mathematics in a deliberate design. While we may not fully comprehend the math behind their construction, they were obviously built with the power of numbers and their relationship to the universe in mind.

Astrology

The stars and planets of the cosmos are powerful. They influence you, contribute to your mood, and impact your fate, and you may not even realize it.

The movement of the stars and their placement in the sky at the time of our births leads to our star signs. This also is true of numerology where our date of birth and the name given to us carries information about our soul and our fate.

In astrology, you have a star sign, and you can divine from this your fate and opportunities. This is commonly referred to as a horoscope, and it operates under the belief that the cosmic alignment of the planets affects our energy. This is a belief shared by numerology and astrology.

In numerology, the same readings can be performed. These are based on your digit sum where a 4 may have a different reading from a 5 or 6 in the same way most people accept that a Sagittarius may have a different energy from a Scorpio.

We know from historians that many examples of numbers and things we would attribute in the modern world to math were studied, built, and recorded by our ancestors. They could build cities from massive stone blocks, yet these cities had perfect geometry and angles.

We see pi in henges and correlations between the stars and monoliths among ancient civilizations. All of this proves that for as long as humanity has existed, we have had a deep and profound relationship with the celestial and the numeric.

Kabbalah

Using similar notions to the Pythagorean numerology, Kabbalah uses the numbers 1 through 9, but it draws solely from an individual's full name, including the middle name, and derives a number from there. While accepted by some, this approach is considered the least accurate among numerologists.

There is also a variation called "new Kabbalah" that uses more modernized ways of divining the meaning of its numbers.

Abracadabra

I had to include this one in our discussion because it does raise some interesting points both about numerology and math.

The least used and possibly most confusing variation of numerology, this discipline uses a more complicated math based around the concept of triangles to discuss its findings.

The reason this is interesting is that researchers who looked into ancient sites have found that advanced math played a role in the building of these older structures, and while the name of this discipline may be silly at first, consider how math may have seemed like magic to the uneducated.

What Is a Numeroscope?

You'll see this term several times throughout this journey, and it is an interesting point of discussion for us to draw attention to. In the everyday world, we will hear people discussing their personality traits as defined by their star signs. Although not everyone believes in the accuracy, it is an accepted part of our everyday life.

In addition to personality traits found in our horoscopes, we will also hear both warnings of compatibility and of duplicity for certain signs, and there are predictions made on a global scale for these identifiers.

In our newspapers and on social media, we can get a horoscope, which is a general outline of the kinds of things that each star sign can expect, as alluded to by the constellations and the celestial bodies.

From love to luck in the big lottery draws, from warnings of sinister threats to predictions of bliss, horoscopes are known to show us many aspects of our lives ahead of when they happen. In a sense, they tell us what will happen in the future.

A numeroscope is the same thing but with the energies and vibrations of the ruling bodies factored in with those of the reader. This is similar to the long-held beliefs that we as people can determine destiny from palm readings or tea leaves.

A numeroscope is a guide, an idea of the kinds of energy influences the universe may have for you and how best to cope with them. Many web pages and social media groups exist for these, so finding one should not be difficult at all.

What Have We Learned?

At the end of each step of our journey together, I want us to look back, review, assess, and reinforce our knowledge.

So far, we have learned that for thousands of years, our ancestors used numbers to divine their fates through the stars and to understand the world around them. Even in the modern world, we see the power of numbers with everything from our phones to our televisions being powered by them.

We have learned that there is a rhythm of numbers in music and that these vibrations are the foundations on which numerology is built. Our names, dates of birth, and even the years we are born in carry this energy, this vibration.

We have learned that, while there are a few variations in the theories and beliefs we hold regarding numbers, the truth is that these have been held for generations.

We have learned that many important, ancient sites used numbers as the source of their power, be it through their positioning or dimensions.

We have learned that not only is it okay to be slightly skeptical, but it is encouraged as things can always be learned by asking more questions.

We have learned about numeroscopes and what information we already get from similar practices in more mainstream thinking. We have begun to see that our fate can be seen if we know where to look.

But what next? In the next chapter, we will begin to unravel the power of numbers first by looking at the value of our digit sums and how they define our energy and our destiny.

The End of Chapter Deep Dive

At the end of each chapter, I will give you a deep dive into a real-world example of a way that you already use numbers, perhaps without realizing it. This first example will be memory cards.

Yes, that is right, SD cards, M2 cards, all of the formats of memory cards display their information using numbers. The capacity is one way, but did you know that all cards have a rating number on them?

This number will likely be on the card itself represented by a number in a circle. This number is a rating, but the rating is more of a compatibility ID, and while all cards can be of good quality, certain numbers benefit different media.

Much like how we will begin to associate the different values of ourselves in numbers, these numbers are already doing this exact thing, and we may not even realize that this is the case.

Chapter 2:

Personality Numbers Part 1

On a scale of one to ten, how would you rate me?

This is a question we have all heard or asked at some point. We value numbers and how we relate to them, and while this isn't strictly reflective of personality numbers, I thought it was an interesting parallel to draw.

You see, dear reader, personality numbers are an important part of our journey together, and while I know at first the idea of having a number or numbers determine who and what we are is an alien concept, it isn't that strange.

The truth is that this is already something we as human beings accept to be true from other, more mainstream ethereal disciplines, such as our star signs. Consider how often you have heard someone explain their behavior away because "they are a Capricorn" or suggest that all Sagittarians have similar personality traits.

Personality numbers, much like star signs, can tell us an awful lot of information about ourselves, information we already try to divine from other sources. This includes information such as if we are letting one part of our true self dominate another. Before we dive into personality numbers, is it best to know exactly what they are.

In this stage of our journey, we will learn what they are and cover the numbers 1 through 4. Here, we will discuss how to determine which personality number applies to you, while also determining what that means to your relationships and the energies around you.

I will then offer some advice on each number toward the end of this chapter, things to try, a little caution perhaps. So, join me as we learn about the first of our personality numbers.

What Are They?

What are personality numbers? This is a simple yet complicated question. Personality numbers are not always something we can control. Instead, they are something chosen for us by fate, by the blueprint of the universe, and while there are some exceptions to this, these are the traits and energies we start with.

From the moment you are born, there are numbers. These numbers, when they relate to your birthday, are the things that your soul will want to explore. They also tell you things about yourself, much like your star sign might tell you; however, these numbers are also a guide.

You'll come to learn that who you are and the energy you have may not match with individuals around you. To understand that more, let's look at the term 'vibe.'

Often, when you hear people discussing a person or situation, you may hear them discuss the 'vibe' they receive from that person. This is the energy or vibration of this person being at odds with the person they are unsure of.

Good vibrations will often come from those around us who have compatible numbers or, at the very least, have compatible traits since some traits are shared by some numbers. For example, you may bond with another intellectual or thrive with another empath.

In this part of our journey, we will look at some of the personality numbers as per Chaldean numerology. Here, we will cover how to work out your personality number and the numbers of anyone else around you. I'll tell you a little about how each of the first four feel and operate, giving you a better understanding of how you fit into the world.

We will discuss the numbers relating to your date of birth and what these can tell you about yourself. You may even come to the realization that you aren't quite living to your maximum potential.

How to Find Personality Numbers

Now that we have established a broader understanding of what a personality number is, we need to know how to find it and how to divine from it our best-laid plans. And that is exactly where our journey takes us now.

To find any personality number, we must first understand that each day has a different energy that is ruled by the digit sum of that day. To work the digit sum out, we must first understand that we tend to look at more than one part of the date of birth to grasp the two personality numbers we all have.

The first number we have to consider is our day of birth. So, for example, you can be a 1 by being born on the 1st, 10th, or 19th of any month. The math here is that 1 on its own is 1, while the 10th becomes 1+0=1 and the 19th becomes 1+9=10, so that, then, means 1+0, again, is 1.

This gives us a digit sum of 1 and shows us the ruling personality number for that date. While these dates are a guide, there are some interesting results, as we will see.

The second of our numbers that determines the personality factor is ruled by the year of someone's birth. For example, if you were born in 1978, the math is 1+9+7+8, which equals 25. And 2+5=7, giving you a digit sum of 7.

This gives you the personality numbers of 1 and 7, which will determine what your soul wants and how your energy vibrates throughout your life. This determines how you can encounter and interact with other people. By giving you the power to understand these numbers, we can start to use that knowledge to better ourselves.

Once we identify the number, its strengths, and its weaknesses, we can better understand things about ourselves that may not have previously made sense. Think of it as a lightbulb moment, a eureka for the soul.

What becomes most interesting is when you compare people to their personality numbers and can start to see where their traits come from. But don't worry, we will come to that later.

Personality Numbers 1 - 4

One

Born on the 1st, 10th, or 19th of any month or in years like 1990 where the digit sum is 1, One represents the beginning. Ones are born leaders and are the first to put their hands up. They are driven to do everything themselves and have a masculine energy.

They can have tendencies to be egotistical, and as a result, they are independent and are prone to dominate most situations.

Along with the potential egotistical streak, Ones can be prone to aggressive behavior. When a One is looking to improve, the core thing they may need to address is this aggressive, egotistical side, embracing instead their leadership qualities and allowing others to come to the fore or learning to delegate.

Ones are generally not keen on manipulating others as they value their freedom highly and, therefore, do not want to take this from others.

Ones will be those who have a hard time wrapping their heads around spiritual ideals and balancing work and social aspects. Ones are singular, loner types, and this can be a difficult trait to remove.

What is interesting is how many examples of power coincide with the number 1. First place in any race or chart is a sought-after position, and while being a One in numerology is not the same thing, it certainly explains the relationship between it and the ego.

Two

Born on the 2nd, 11th, 20th, and 29th of any month and in years like 2000 where the digit sum is 2, Twos are ostensibly the parallel to Ones, being collaborators.

Twos are, by nature, a feminine energy. They are fun and joyous, almost playful people. Empathetic to the emotions of others, they are creative with their drive leaning toward the concept of fun at the core.

Twos often absorb too much emotion from others, with their gentleness often seen as a weakness by those around them. But don't be fooled; this emotional depth is a strength—a strength that needs refining yes, but a strength all the same.

With their pronounced spiritual side and their proneness to absorbing all of the excess energy from others around them, Twos need to work mostly on themselves, their boundaries, and protecting their needs. This may be tough for these gentle empaths, but it will help them to grow out of traps they may have fallen into, such as being a crutch for others.

Three

Threes are born on the 3rd, 12th, 21st, and 30th of any month or in years like 1983 where the digit sum is 3. Threes are creative, entrepreneurial types who are the concepts of manifestation and expansion.

Threes appreciate art and creativity. They enjoy learning and reading and are driven by the strength to follow through. They have a thirst for success, often exploring new ideas, creating solutions, and leading, but in a nuanced way.

Great communicators, Threes are capable of increasing the belief in others, but they are prone to overexertion and often need to learn to take breaks as sometimes they can suffer from intense tunnel vision.

While Threes are seen to be intuitive people who adapt quickly to situations, they are, thanks to that tunnel vision I mentioned, prone to overthinking, overanalysis, and becoming fixated on a specific issue.

The concept of 'action' at the core of who a Three is can become problematic if they don't learn to remove themselves from this way of behaving.

There is a cell phone company in the UK called 3. Their advertisements are bright, vibrant, and often creative. This company can be seen everywhere, and the relationship between the number 3 and the energy of the Three here is no mistake.

Four

Fours are born on the 4th, 13th, 22nd, or 31st of every month and any year where the digit sum is 4, for example, 1966. This number is representative of change or overcoming something.

Fours are rebellious, the revolutionaries, the out-of-the-box thinkers who work toward the future. These innovators are keen on forethought and on planning and adapting to the different situations they interact in.

Fours are also seen as self-disciplined, keeping themselves in order, clutter-free as it were. This is manifested in the world outside them where they revolt against disorder and look toward unity and structure.

Fours consider themselves defined not by the company they keep but instead by the groups they avoid. However, this can prove an issue for Fours as they struggle with developing and maintaining relationships.

Fours should be looking for kindred spirits and breaking their rigorous shell as they can become so ingrained in their pursuits that they lose track of who and what is important to them.

Where do you sit so far? We have other numbers to cover, yes, but do these apply to you? Are you surprised? When we started the journey together, did you feel that some part of your soul was unfulfilled?

Don't be alarmed; surprises are coming in this journey. These surprises will give us a new perspective, a new understanding.

This new understanding we are gaining together is the reason we started this journey. When we see something as simple as needing more emotional freedom or we experience more boundaries against us, as defined by our birth, it can make a lot of sense, especially if we have felt incomplete in our lives.

This is why this journey is so important. We need to embrace and understand ourselves on a more spiritual, deeper level.

For the next step, dear reader, I wanted to offer some advice to show what things you can try as each of these numbers to enrich your life.

If you are realizing you are a One who perhaps hasn't had the chance to be a leader, find local groups and become involved in arranging events. This will allow you to learn your skills while also allowing you to make mistakes, something Ones are normally pretty afraid of. It is also important as a One to not be afraid of making mistakes in general, so the practice of trying without this fear is good.

If you have had leadership opportunities, maybe you already knew you were a One but were wondering how to broaden your skills. Reach out to more empathetic types and ask them for their point of view on the situations at hand. Leading is a great skill to have, but having the right advice will help you to no end.

Ones can also benefit from working with leaders from other numbers. However, Ones need to allow others to take the forefront. Stepping back and following can help a One to balance that drive to always be in the lead.

For Twos, I would recommend channeling all of the emotional energy, the spiritual baggage, into something. Find a creative outlet that suits you; it could be something like writing or music or drawing. Even if those things are things you are learning for the first time, allowing yourself to express yourself can help unburden much of that excess energy you've accumulated.

Twos can also benefit greatly from meditation by allowing themselves to unburden the negative energies that they may have accumulated from others. Finding the right routines and rituals—anything from meditation to rearranging the furniture and energy of a room—can be helpful, giving them an emotional outlet in a controlled way.

If you are reading this and part of your personality is a Two and you have difficulty expressing yourself emotionally, it may be that you have always been discouraged from doing so. This is especially true of men where the stigma in society is so strong. You will need to learn to embrace this emotional side as it will better help you to destress and relax.

Very empathetic numbers like Twos can flourish around creative numbers and often feel things more profoundly than others, so embarking on conversations can help Twos to better express themselves.

Threes need to apply their love of learning to a love of rigorous structure. If you are a Three, giving yourself breaks is so important. It could be that you are exhausted, so making specific time to allow yourself to switch off will be vitally important.

Find a hobby or give yourself the time to stand still. This is something that I cannot fully expand the importance of, and it is something you must work on as a Three. Expression and the self are especially important if you are a Three and a Two as you will carry that emotional depth in addition to the creative need.

As a Three, seek out leadership types and find ways to be creative in the projects or ideas. Lending your creativity to a new outlet can be immensely rewarding with the onus on a larger goal than just the creating itself.

For Fours, those issues with making friendships and connections could come from low self-esteem. I'd look at how you treat and think of yourself. Making some changes to your inner dialogue will allow you to feel connections much easier than you currently do.

Another way to help build those bridges is to join social media groups for things you enjoy. Be it gaming, music, movies, or even board games, there are groups for all interests out there, and using those things as conversation starters can lead to building bridges.

Putting together groups can also be achieved via project planning where the different parties can bounce ideas off of one another with you able to add your energy with less of the stigma of being rejected.

Numbers That Complement

While you may think it is as simple as a One having great vibrations with another One, the truth is a little more complicated. While a One's energy will mesh well with other Ones, the truth is that often, leaders will clash with leaders. The best matches are people who share traits but also have opposing energies. For example, a One and a Nine (which we will cover more in the next chapter) both have leadership qualities; however, Ones are quite intent on being about the self, while Nines are more emotive and capable of following.

They are, therefore, complemented by energies that are happy to compromise. Now, this doesn't mean that Ones always should get their way. In fact, often, challenging them can benefit them to no end by giving them a new perspective that is helpful.

While we can all have multiple energies, the dominant traits we have determine who we complement. This is especially true if we have similar energies in both of our personality numbers.

What Have We Learned?

Throughout this stage of our journey, we have learned what personality numbers are and how we would go about working out our personality number based on our day and year of birth.

We have had an in-depth look at numbers 1 through 4, the things they represent, and the things those numbers can work on. We know which days of the month apply to these numbers and even have examples of some years so that we can see how the digit sum math works.

I also offered some advice on things to consider for each of the various numbers, especially if you haven't known until this journey which personality number defines you.

We have looked at a couple of examples of the kind of complement our number provides us and the way our dominant personalities can bring out our best.

But the truth is, dear reader, we have a long way left to go. There are many miles left to travel before we can finally say we have reached our journey's end. We have many things left to cover and many ideas to discuss.

The End of Chapter Deep Dive

Time for the second example of numbers we already know about in our daily lives: review scores. You probably don't realize the power behind these because of how common they are.

Review scores are everywhere and exist for everything. Normally rated out of 5, 10, or 100, we score and separate the various content we digest into scores, both as an arbitrary way of scaling its value or quality and also because we know that someone can look at a score and have a rough idea of what to expect from that piece of media.

Some reviews even break down certain aspects of the end product. Consider the example of a film. There may be a score for the lighting, acting, or plot. Even the monster in a horror movie could be reviewed and scored in this way, allowing for those who are interested in those elements of an experience to be aware that, while the plot is 'bad,' the monster is 'good' and, therefore, still worth the investment.

We review things as a way of attributing their value to us, yes, but we also do this as a way of communicating through numbers. But do you know what else happens with reviews?

We disagree, a lot, on social media, on forums, by the watercooler. Anytime the idea of a review score comes up, it invariably creates a disagreement, both because of how people view the media in question and how the number makes them feel in relation to the scoring system.

Many times, you may look at a film that has scored a 6 or a 7 out of 10 and feel yourself uncomfortable with that score for that film, instead, thinking that the film deserved a higher or lower score.

This discomfort and the way the numbers affect you specifically are similar sensations to the energies of someone else or the cosmos throwing your vibrations out of sync.

Interestingly, many review sites have begun to move away from numerical numbering systems. Some have managed to better hide the exact way they attribute the number in these cases, but sometimes, it is still apparent.

Star rating systems are often a replacement for "out of 5" systems, although if half measurements are included, this could be seen as an "out of 10" system.

We also see these numbers in grading. Many European countries grade on numbers, and the UK recently moved from a letter-grade system to a number system. Grades are a measurement of success derived from the letter grade or number grade. It is determined by other numbers, usually percentages, that make up the output of the student.

And much like film review scores, these arbitrary grades will follow students for a long time after their departure from formal education and are how many people will judge them.

Chapter 3:

Personality Numbers Part 2

Now that we have covered the first four personality numbers, as well as how to calculate these, it is time to move on to the remainder of the numbers. In this stage of our journey together, we will look at numbers 5 through 9, discussing their strengths and weaknesses, and I'll be offering a little advice for each.

We will also take time to look at several famous people and their personality numbers. From the view of what is surprising and what is not, we will discuss which of the various traits that we see connected to the energies of these numbers have helped this person achieve greatness.

We will give several examples of the math we use, the digit sums, so that this form of thinking can become more natural to discuss. We will also use these examples as a way of showing that, while some traits are likely to clash, a healthy approach to balance can help us achieve anything.

We will even take a look at a couple of fictional examples that will allow us to look at if these energies are considered in the development of characters.

Personality Numbers 5 - 9

Five

Fives are born on the 5th, 14th, and 23rd of each month and in years where the digit sum is 5, like 1994. They are connection-driven communicators at heart.

Fives have high energy and thrive in jobs like sales or while juggling lots of deadlines, seemingly blossoming under pressure.

They prefer working with more grounded individuals. Fives like to travel, feeding into their high energy. They also are magnetic, charismatic, and adapt well to changes.

Fives do, however, run the risk of being too stretched or becoming distracted from personal interaction due to the sheer volume of things they are doing. So, it is important for them to take time to switch off the noise and take a well-earned breather.

Six

Sixes are people born on the 6th, 15th, or 24th of the month or people whose birth year has the digit sum of 6, for example, 1977. This is the number most associated with love, harmony, and teaching.

Sixes are drawn to beauty but not just in a fashion sense. They notice the balance of the world and the harmony and serenity of things. They often make excellent counselors, teaching others both in the literal and spiritual sense.

They often feel responsible for the community they foster since they are caring and personable, needing to learn to love inwardly as well as outwardly.

They can also be blinded by their compassion and often need to learn it is okay to walk away from a toxic situation.

Seven

Sevens are born on the 7th, 16th, and 25th of every month and in years with a digit sum of 7, much like our earlier example of 1978. Sevens are our spiritual sponges, the ones with insight into the metaphysical and philosophical.

Sevens will be the type of person to always have another question, another way of seeing the world and all its mysteries. They are daydreamers who can be artistic but also can work well with others.

It is here that a Seven needs to be careful, however, as they can be prone to lacking the willpower of other, more dominant types. Often, Sevens will need some alone time to put their thoughts in order and construct their understanding.

Sevens need to trust their gut instinct or intuition more so that they can better capitalize on their ability to bring their understanding of the cosmos to the fore.

Eight

Eights are born on the 8th, 17th, and 26th of the month and in years such as 1997. This is the number that draws the most tumultuous of energies, being driven by challenge and constant motion.

Eights are often driven by success or power, both on the physical and metaphysical scale, and can, as a consequence, seem temperamental, but this is simply misplaced passion.

Eights will have a good grasp of how to control their power, but they may struggle with their self-worth if things are not going their way. Eights need to temper their expectations.

Eights can be found constantly moving and searching, even in the darkness itself, for their answers. What do they seek? Authenticity and recognition. Eights have a lot of potential, but they are the numbers who struggle with their inner balance the most.

Nine

Nines are born on the 9th, 18th, and 27th of any month and in any year where the digit sum is 9, like 1980. This number is a number of completion, the most well-rounded number with elements of each of the other numbers.

While Nines can be leaders, it is done with their hearts firmly on their sleeves. They have the steel to be fighters and are usually quick to point out injustice.

Nines are compassionate, patient, and kind. They have a vast emotional spectrum and, as such, can leave themselves vulnerable to the stresses of the world, resulting in common headaches.

The number itself is seen as divine and a symbol of completion.

Advice for 5 - 9

Now, we have covered the remainder of our personality numbers. Let's take the time to talk about some of the lessons we can learn about these numbers and how they can apply to us. If they are us, we can talk about how best to address the feelings of incompleteness we may be experiencing.

For Fives, the advice is always going to be to find that balance between who you are on the spiritual level and how much time you give to any one thing. Taking short breaks is good, but you need to understand that overstraining the soul is only going to be harmful in the long run.

I'd suggest setting alarms on your phone so that you can have your break times at the same time where possible. The constant motion is great in bursts, so making time to do something silly or soothing will help Fives with their balance.

It is also worth noting that holidays and rest breaks are not just good for the soul; they are also good for the body. Tension is a real problem for those who are always on the go, and Fives are going to need to find ways to ease that tension where possible.

Sixes need to learn to receive the praise and love they share. This is something that can be incredibly difficult for Sixes, so making positive reinforcement a personal growth goal can and will be hugely beneficial.

Perhaps write down a list of things that you don't like about yourself, and then begin a list of things that you think you are good at or do well. This can help grow your critical assessment skills and purge some of those negative thoughts.

Sevens need to work on the here and now and living in the moment as they can be quite prone to 'flighty' behavior. Savoring moments while experiencing them is of huge importance. Trusting their intuition will also be a big gain.

A diary or planner can be a great tool used to plan for the future. It is also great for noting the things you have done. Scrapbooks are a good way to encourage living in the now since photos make for good moments.

Eights are the ones who have to learn how to let go of the baggage. They carry a lot of pressure and challenges in an internalized way, and they need to learn to jettison some of this excess to get themselves back on the right track by remembering that the weight isn't just on them.

Burning mementos of bad times can be the best action for an Eight. When done safely, this is a cathartic exercise that allows the baggage to be let go of and the low to feed into an emotional high.

Nines are in an interesting position. While they have some of the same traits as all of the other numbers, the problem they often have is being an exposed nerve while trying to be everything to everyone. This is something that is potentially quite harmful.

Much like other emotional types, meditation is important for Nines. It allows them to clear their minds of all of the noise and influences around them.

What Should You Do If Your Numbers Clash?

One question you may have is what to do if your personality numbers clash. The truth is that the answer is simple. We all have two personality numbers. For example, the first may have aspects of leadership and learning, while the other may be emotional and creative.

The way these may clash is that the emotional burden of leading may be too much for your creative side. The way to resolve this would be to reconcile the differences.

As with many things in our lives, the answer is balance. In this example, our would-be leader may be feeling overwhelmed as they lack the knowledge they feel they need, so adjusting their balance to this new way of being can help restore the energy of clashing numbers.

If the elements of your numbers are order and rebellion, this can be balanced by having a routine five days a week during a working structure and then the freedom to express your rebellious side the remaining time. Balance is the answer when we ask about clashing personality types.

It is a simple yet complex answer because while balance will vary from number to number, it is a simple process of introspection. You need to ask yourself which elements of which parts of who you are frighten you. This is where the balance lies. Therefore, focusing on other complementing traits can help redress this balance.

Famous Examples

For a change of pace, we are going to do something a little more fun here. We are going to look at several famous people and their personality numbers based on what we have discussed and see what traits we can easily identify within the individuals in question.

We can then better see what skills and strengths each personality brings out. This allows for people to be far more successful than they might otherwise have expected. Keep in mind that not every trait from a number applies to every person with that number.

These numbers will also give a better understanding of the power of numbers, and once we begin to apply this to ourselves, we can start to better determine what elements of our soul we are not using to the fullest.

David Bowie

David Bowie, real name David Jones, was a British singer famous for his peculiar lyrics and outlandish presentation who had a career spanning decades with successful albums and singles the world over.

David Bowie has the base numbers of 8 and 3, with Threes being associated with the arts and creativity and Eights being driven to succeed. This combination is hardly surprising for a person who often created music in a unique way and went on to such grand success.

Did you know, for example, that Bowie would write lyrics then shuffle them until they resonated with him in a better way? Interestingly, Bowie was completely in tune with how things would resonate with him, and to look at his legacy, it certainly resonated with others too.

David Bowie was also an accomplished actor, appearing in the movie *Labyrinth*, a performance still talked about and heavily praised to this day.

Barack Obama

Barack Obama was the 44th president of the United States. He came to embody hope and change, becoming a spokesperson for equality and change since leaving office.

Obama's numbers are a 4 and an 8, so what can we learn from this? Well, Eights are associated with taking on challenges, passion, power, and authenticity.

Even with a cursory glance, this is Obama to the letter, but when partnered with the other number in his personality, the tale becomes ever clearer. With Obama being a number 4, we can see he is a revolutionary with a drive to bring order to chaos. He is also an out-of-the-box thinker.

With these two elements, we can see the reflection of the Obama we know from his time in office and the changes he brought to the United States.

Paul Pogba

World Cup winner and global megastar soccer player, Paul Pogba, from France, is a young man with the world at his feet. One of the most expensive soccer players ever signed, Pogba commanded a fee of over 100 million euros (almost 120 million dollars) to move to Manchester United from Juventus in 2016.

Pogba's numbers are a 6 and a 4. Sixes have traits related to community responsibility and fashion sense, both of which have been big parts of Pogba's character both at a club and international level.

The number 4 is also a good fit for Pogba. His career at Manchester United has been fraught with issues pertaining to his rebellious nature; however, for France, Pogba has shown a great balance of leadership and maturity, which has not always been shown at the club level. This is a testament to that delicate balance Fours must try to strike.

Bill Gates

Bill Gates, the former owner of Microsoft, comes in with a personality combination of the numbers 1 and 2, which is an interesting combination as there are several clashes that could have happened. Ones are leaders, the first through a door, and this kind of market leadership is what Gates and Microsoft were known for.

Famously, Bill Gates was turned down for a job with Apple and went on to success anyway, which is also indicative of a One since they love to succeed on their own. With Microsoft being a computing juggernaut in the modern world, it is safe to say he did succeed.

Where we see the Two in Bill Gates's personality is the charity work and giving he has been at the center of since stepping away from Microsoft, which shows his empathetic side, coupled with the creativity we saw from him in his career.

It would have been quite easy for Gates to struggle to balance these aspects of his personality, yet he has found the balance to let each have its time, and this is an important lesson for us to make use of. Balance and patience feed into all of our decisions.

Oprah Winfrey

Much like Bill Gates, Oprah Winfrey is both a Two and a One. To say that Oprah is just empathetic, emotionally flexible, creative, and receptive to her world would be the greatest understatement of all.

But as much as she is clearly a Two, she also is a leader, someone who sets the example she wants to see in others, leading by making use of her understanding of the emotional spectrum.

Oprah is also an accomplished actress, having starred in the film *The Color Purple*, among other projects. This shows the creative and flexible nature she has embedded in her soul. She's a different kind of creative from Bill Gates for sure.

Oprah and Bill serve as interesting parallels, both being Twos and Ones. Their end goals are so different, yet what drives their personalities is similar. Oprah shows us that we can have elements of the positive side of our personality numbers without always having to compromise as she can often be seen doing multiple projects at once.

Lady Gaga

Lady Gaga, real name Stefani Germanotta, is both a Three and a Six. Sixes focus on beauty and harmony and can appreciate the world for what it is and embrace it, which seems fitting for a musician.

What is even more fitting for Lady Gaga is that she is a Three, the number that shows strength and the thirst to succeed. If you know anything of Lady Gaga's career, you will know before she reinvented herself, Stefani was rejected by record labels, so she fought for her passion, showing her strength of character to succeed above all.

This is especially inspiring when you see how well Lady Gaga has taken to acting in the movie *A Star Is Born* and the TV series *American Horror Story* where she gets to express those creative energies in a new way.

KT Tunstall

KT Tunstall, real name Kate Tunstall, is a Scottish singer and songwriter, and her numbers are 5 and 4.

Fours are rebellious, and Fives are high energy, and both of these traits seem extremely fitting for a musician, especially one who draws inspiration from women like Joan Jett. Both KT and Joan have the base numbers 4 and 5. Perhaps the inspiration drawn by KT is because she sees Joan as a kindred spirit—the numbers certainly indicate as much.

KT is also a great spokesperson for the arts and is often found sharing her energies with charities and events she feels connections to, tapping into her emotional and spiritual need to rebel against injustice where she sees it.

Fictional Examples

I thought it might be fun to touch on a couple of famous fictional examples. One is probably a little more famous than the other, but both are interesting, and with their birthday information written into their characters, we can look at how personality numbers are reflected in these characters and determine if, just maybe, this was intentional.

While my sample group is small, this is something I am sure people who create influential characters consider when they include birthdays.

Harry Potter

Born to destiny as the protagonist and hero of the series of novels, Harry was born on June 31, 1980, which gives him the numbers 4 and 9.

Nines are shown to have leadership qualities and have their hearts firmly on their sleeves, which we know is evident in the character of Harry Potter.

Fours are the out-of-the-box thinkers and rebels; anyone who has read the book series will know that this also applies to Harry.

Were these elements chosen deliberately? It is hard to argue definitively. But there does seem to be some evidence of this since we know J.K. Rowling has been said to have researched aspects for all of the elements of her books to make them "feel real." Perhaps this is a reflection of that?

Superman

Superman was born Kal-El on the planet Krypton. There is a slight snag with his number, though.

Superman has several conflicting dates of birth due to the longevity of the character, so I figured we would instead use the first publication date for Superman, which is April 18, 1938, making him a Nine and Three.

Nine would make Superman a compassionate leader, a trait we have seen time and again throughout the history of the media featuring the Man of Steel.

In my breakdown of what a Three is, I used the following phrase: "Threes are capable of increasing the belief in others." If this does not personify the last son of Krypton, I don't know what does.

Were these intentional? It is impossible to say, but it certainly seems so, knowing what we know.

What Have We Learned?

Now, we have covered all of the personality numbers, their underlying principles, and the lessons we can learn from them. We have also taken the time to look at key elements of advice for each of the numbers, and we even had a look at a few successful and influential celebrities.

We looked at which elements of their personality numbers could be attributed to their success. We also learned that fictional characters can have the same kinds of energies in their dates of birth or original publication date and that elements of these energies can feed into what the character becomes iconic for.

So, we now have a far clearer understanding of what numerology is and how to figure out the value of a date and year of birth, but our journey still has many places and names to see.

Before we move on, pause for a moment. What numbers rule your life? Using digit sum calculations, add the day of your birth together and the year. Which numbers are you?

If you find that these numbers are at odds with one another, this may be contributing to internal conflict, but as we have begun to see, there is a way around those feelings. It is also possible that you have the same personality number twice, emphasizing the core traits in you.

The End of Chapter Deep Dive

When we think of numbers, we often think of these grand, complicated things, things that are bigger than us, but the truth is they aren't always. Often, these ideas are far, far smaller.

Our deep dive here is our diet. Yes, you read that right. If you have in the past or are currently dieting, you'll know that all diets work with numbers, although you may not have realized the correlation until now. What number is it? It is a number we use all of the time, but we probably never see its influence and power over us. This number is a calorie.

While each diet differs from the other in some ways, they all have calories as the driving force. But what is a calorie?

A calorie is a measurement of energy, and through science, we can determine how much of this energy is in the food or fluids we consume. We then know how much of this energy the body needs for sustenance, how much we are burning, and what the leftover elements are. Through this, we can better gauge how to lose weight or how much we would need to consume to put on weight for bulking up.

Many diets convert the calorie content of food into points, allowing people a certain number of points per day, and while these numbers are not assigned a good or bad ratio, we can still understand what they mean to us as the person using the diet.

It is interesting that we know that numbers and energy go hand in hand in this way and that we can scientifically measure that same energy. It is also interesting that we can draw meaning from numbers outside of their more traditional uses.

This is what numerology is, the idea of the influence of numbers on our soul. If we think of the practices we are widely discussing as a diet plan for the soul, it'll make a lot of sense. We are looking at what things the soul needs to consume to thrive. That's all numerology is at its core, and that is some food for thought.

Chapter 4:

Letters and Numbers Part 1

Names are already important to us. They are part of what defines us, even those of us who have similar names. We name our children, our pets, and even our cars. Names appear on houses, boats, planes, and even trucks. Names hold a power that we accept as people, but do we know where this power comes from?

Much like the day and year in which we are born, there is a great amount of information about us that we can ascertain from our names. The base numbers of our names are elements that supplement the information we have drawn from our personality numbers to look further into ourselves and begin to understand and maximize our potential.

This potential is the reason we are drawn to certain names and why there are common, popular names. We see the energies of that name and the opportunities that it creates. This is why people pick personalized license plates and why some people change their given names.

This is also, adversely, why some names fall out of use because the energy of that name is not resonating with people in the way it used to. There is also an interesting phenomenon that you have likely experienced at least once in your life, and this is the phenomenon where someone will tell you their name, and it doesn't feel right.

These things are as much about the energy of the names themselves as they are about the value of the energy names create. That is the next stage of our journey together.

In this chapter, we will begin to learn about names, the power they hold, and how changing your name can lead to a difference in power. We will also see how names can be temporary and how our soul knows if our name is wrong.

How to Work Out the Energy of a Name

Much like with the date and year of birth from the previous chapters, the ruling energy of a name is determined by its digit sum. This is worked out differently than the way we calculate dates; however, as we will see shortly, we need to first ascertain the various values of each letter, which is a system that we will come to see is quite common.

Now, the common assumption is that the system would work with the letter A being the letter with the corresponding value of the number 1. It would continue this way until Z, which would have a value of 26. However, this is not correct. For our math, all letters are assigned to the numbers 1 through 8. The number 9 is an exception. It is not a ruler of any of the letters, but a name can belong to 9 and the energies it creates. We will look more at this exception in Chapter 5.

To get the digit sum, each of the respective digits is added together and together again until, as with the personality number, we are given a singular digit between 1 and 9. Unlike our personality numbers, this number is also our planetary ruler.

For example, say you have the name Joy. If you add numbers for the letters J, O, and Y together, you come to their digit sum, which is 9, as our calculation is 1+7+1.

What we will come to learn is that if the name and the person's personality number share a trait, this trait is often emphasized, becoming a dominant trait in that individual.

Numbers 1 - 4 and What They Rule

So, we begin the road to full enlightenment with more questions. Which numbers command which letters? Which planets are we discussing?

Here, we will begin to look at each number in turn with a few points about what we know of the number as divined from a name. We will also have a look at which celestial body governs them, and for each number, we will give an example of a name that will fall under this number. I will use an example name for each number, but the traits we discuss will apply to all names with that digit number.

I'll also offer some activities for each number, which are things to try to help balance this aspect of the self. This includes things like meditation and creative projects. Even yelling into the night might appear here.

One

In regards to a name, the number 1 covers five letters, these letters being A, I, J, Q, and Y. Much like with our personality number, this can be reached with digit sums that add up to 10 or 19 since you cannot have a name that is 1 on its own.

One is the Sun, the solar, the star in the sky. This is an energy that is a doer, an active force in the world, and it is driven to be both innovative and original as much as possible. Ones are often accused of having bossy and impatient traits, but this, too, can be used to their benefit.

One is, like with the personality number, seen as masculine, and it tends to be suited to people who enjoy business ventures.

Name Example: Dan, 4+1+5=10, 1+0=1

As we can see here, the name Dan creates the digit sum of 1, and it is the first example of why how someone identifies themselves should also be considered as part of their digit sum.

Let me explain. In this instance, our Dan is identifying his energy as a One, dropping what he sees as the excess letters from his name (presumably Daniel) to make it feel more natural. People who do this may not even realize that this change of name is something their soul needed due to the energy in their personal blueprint.

Ones may want to try several small tasks. Many also are business people at heart. Something that I think might be helpful, especially for the more independent Ones out there, is to make a spreadsheet on their computer and begin to track their income and expenses. This will engage that entrepreneur part of their soul, allowing that aspect of who they are shine.

A Dan with the personality number of 1 may have a dominant personality of leadership, making this person ideal for project leadership or for starting a company. However, in this instance, he should be especially careful with how he interacts with others as he could potentially become too heavy-handed.

What is interesting is when someone who is named Daniel changes their name to Dan. We will see a few more instances of this in the numbers to come. This changes the energy of the name. Changing it to Danny also changes the energy. This is likely something the individual doesn't realize is being shown to them by the universe.

Two

Two covers B, K, and R and, like the number 2 from our personality number calculations, is the digit sum for any name that comes to 2.

Two is the Moon, the lunar, and like Twos from the personality number, it is feminine, patient and caring, sensitive and creative. Twos are often accused of being prone to mood swings, but again, this isn't always a bad thing when tempered with the right preparation and insight.

The balance for Twos will always be tempering that inner need to heal others with the boundaries set by other people. Some of the more independent numbers will try to retain boundaries that Twos may not like, but this is part of the learning process for a Two.

Name Example: Matthew, $4+1+4+4+5+5+6=29$, $2+9=11$, $1+1=2$

While the short version of Matthew, Matt, is a 4, the full version is a 2, so if and when you meet someone who doesn't like to abbreviate their name, it could simply be that the abridged version of the name doesn't vibrate with them spiritually.

If I had to suggest anything for a Two, it would be to volunteer. Volunteering is a great way to channel that caring, healing energy into something positive. Even if it is just once a month, give yourself that outlet where your caring nature can be appreciated.

For our Matthew, if their personality number is also 2, they may find that they are affected by the cosmos on an emotional level more than most, and this is where the outlets for this energy are most important.

It is also important to note that this energy can lead to others believing you are a pushover, so those boundaries are the most important in this case.

Three

Three covers C, G, L, and S. The number 3 falls under the planet Jupiter and is a creative, clever, and lucky number. This number is generally excitable, extroverted, and charming.

However, there are pitfalls, which are being too chatty and easily distracted with a lack of discipline. There is also a chance that this kind of energy can lead to narcissism.

Threes do, however, like to put themselves out there. They are the performers and dancers of the world, taking center stage whenever they can.

Example Name: Theo, 4+5+5+7=21, 2+1=3

Theo is an energetic, extroverted name. Even the way this name sounds can be exciting for us. Interestingly, the much longer version of this name, Theodore, has a digit sum of 3 as well, while the common nickname Teddy has a digit sum of 9, giving it a different energy.

For Threes, I recommend writing a blog or reviews, something to allow you to discuss and present your feelings on a wide range of topics. This will satisfy your inner entertainer, and you'll find if you are quite chatty, this kind of analysis will suit you well.

For our friend Theo, if his personality number is 3, he may, at times, be overly charged with energy, feeling almost manic. This can lead to crashes, leading him to fall flat, so it is of the utmost importance that he expresses himself in a way that can be done in stages.

If you are a Three, plans or short bursts of activities will help you to no end. A good thing to try is to put break reminders in your calendar. Small breaks for a few minutes (say 5 to 10 minutes) a few times a day will allow your brain the chance to process things.

Four

Four covers the letters D, M, and T and falls under the planet Uranus. Fours can be intelligent, with an emphasis on loyalty at their core.

They are tenacious and driven by facts and details, so they may seem stubborn or overly opinionated, but this just stems from them wanting things done to their standard.

It's the loyalty that tends to cause the issues that Fours have with letting go. They feel that by letting go, they are letting down their peers, not realizing that they will need to let go to benefit the self and the soul.

Example Name: Will, 6+1+3+3=13, 1+3=4

Will is a 4; William, however, would be a 1, and I draw attention to this for a reason.

One of the themes we have to cover throughout our journey together is the idea of making changes to better embrace and control the energy around us. Much like the example of Dan before, people who identify as a Will have a different energy than those who identify as a William, and this has everything to do with the energy of the name.

For Wills who are our number 4, they risk being too rigid in their thinking. Listening to others and trying new techniques regularly is something that Wills and other Fours will need to do to help keep on top of their energy.

While it is okay to be the smartest person in a room, no one is right all of the time, and learning to accept when you are wrong can be an important skill.

Famous Examples

Here, we are going to take a moment to look at some famous people who either have a digit sum of the numbers we have discussed in this section or the same names we used in the examples. I am hoping that this will show that names, much like dates of birth and the personality numbers therein, can influence our success.

Our first famous Dan and the first famous One in this section that we will have a look at is Dan Reynolds, the lead singer of Imagine Dragons, a rock band from Los Angeles. Dan is clearly driven to be innovative and original, as the rock-and-roll lifestyle often dictates.

The second famous Dan we will discuss is one you'll know, but it may not be immediately clear as to where you know him from. Dan Castellaneta's voice is known to millions around the world as the voice of Homer Simpson. Like our first Dan, this Dan also uses the creative energy he takes from his digit sum of 1.

For famous Matthews and famous Twos, we are spoiled for choice with Matthew McConaughey, Matthew Perry, and Matthew Morrison, who are all good examples.

It is interesting that all three of these Matthews are actors and can most often be seen expressing emotion and drama through their acting. In fact, there is an element that shows the truest of expressions here, as all of the Matthews can be seen in comedies, serious dramas, and on stage, with Matthew Morrison being famous for his musical role in the TV show *Glee*.

Moving on to Threes and famous Theos or Theodores, we have Theodore Roosevelt, who was the 26th president of the United States. He was clever and articulate but also suffered from frustration.

Roosevelt ran for the presidential nomination in 1912 after he was previously in office. He failed, however, so he went on an expedition to the Amazon Rainforest.

Roosevelt showed his intelligent side in his understanding of naval tactics that he learned from studying books on the matter at Harvard University. This shows his thirst for knowledge.

Will Smith is a famous Four and a famous Will. He is clearly an intelligent and tenacious man. He has not only forged himself a successful multimedia career, but he has also demonstrated that he is a loyal man, having shown loyalty to the friends he became famous with from the projects that defined his past.

Cognitive Dissonance

As I touched on in the introduction to this chapter, there is a sensation that applies to us human beings that I believe stems from energy but for which there is a scientific explanation.

The example I used was the feeling of unease that stems from a person telling you their name and a wrongness vibrating through you. This sensation and others like it are cognitive dissonance.

This occurs when the experience you are having is at odds with your knowledge and experience or when someone offers information that conflicts with the things you believe or feel.

In regards to how this relates to numerology, we experience this sensation at times when the vibration and energies we are receiving from a person are reacting to us in a way we do not expect or cannot explain. It could be that the individual in question is in the grips of something like personal turmoil, or there could be simpler explanations.

This person may identify as a name that doesn't vibrate with you in the way that you would anticipate. This could be because you get a different vibe from them. They could identify as an Andy, but you get a vibe from them that feels closer to an Andrew.

This kind of feeling can be curtailed by clearing other factors and then asking this person if you can call them Andrew rather than Andy.

This can act as an interesting counterpoint to when we feel something is just right, that moment of clarity and bliss that occurs when all of the things fall into place, a feeling called an epiphany. This would be the exact opposite of that particular sensation.

What Have We Learned?

We have begun to cover the value of the letters within our names, the value we carry with us in our lives, a part of the fabric that defines who we are, and why. But how can we begin to apply what we have learned?

When we look at a name with a digit sum of 1, for a person who is born on a date that also has a digit sum of 1, we can see that this person has a big drive to become a leader.

If the person's name and the numbers we draw from it clash idealistically, what can we draw from it?

While we will cover this as our journey advances, we can certainly start to consider the question. We can also ask ourselves if this is why people use stage names or change their real names.

Names like Daniel, Matthew, Jonathan, William, Elizabeth, and many others can be abbreviated, tweaked, and changed; however, this isn't always what the person wants. I have known Matthews who want to be called Matthew, clearly identifying with that name and its energies.

The End of Chapter Deep Dive

The journey we are on doesn't have a map that you can hold, although I guess you could call this book a map of sorts. Real maps, though, have numbers, grid references, and coordinates.

These numbers help us travel, and they help us determine our best path or the best way for us to navigate from one end of a town to another, from one building in a city to another.

And these coordinates are universal. We map space, the movement of the stars, and the planets themselves using coordinates, using numbers.

We begin to see that numbers rule journeys. From the speed of a car to how much fuel is in the tank, from when we leave to the time we need to arrive, we think of all journeys in numbers.

Returning to bus, subway, and train times, these inform our journeys as much as the things we directly control since they are the numbers by which we structure the journey as route, flight, ticket, and seat numbers.

All of these numbers feed into our ability to travel and the world's ability to move around us. They also enable the universe to move around the world and so on and so on.

It is a fact that all journeys in the physical can be measured in numbers, even life. We know the lifespan of bugs, the amount of time they have to metamorphosize, and the time until they perish.

We think in these ways all of the time without realizing it. Is it so different to have the journey of our soul and our energy measured in numbers?

Chapter 5:

Letters and Numbers Part 2

In this chapter of our journey together, we can start to look at the remaining numbers, their rules, and what they represent. We will also take the time to discuss the planets themselves and how celestial movements can affect not only our souls but also the very world around us. We will talk about the effect of planets on our energy and how best to plan for negative and positive effects.

Numbers 5 - 9 and What They Rule

Once again, we will discuss these numbers, but we will also ask ourselves some important questions, including what happens when someone changes their name, not as a nickname, but as an outright change?

There are many examples of this, and in this section, we will discuss how and why this happens, but first, let's look at the remaining ruling numbers.

Five

Five is the number of Mercury and contains the letters E, H, N, and X for sums. This number is a number that lives free, is communicative and intelligent, and is driven by a more masculine vibration.

There are, however, some self-serving aspects of Fives. There is a potential addict's personality under the veneer, so this number needs to be calm and more responsible in how they act toward others.

Example Name: Ines, 1+5+5+3=14, 1+4=5

Free-willed and intelligent for a name that has its origins in Spanish-speaking countries, this seems pertinent for a culture defined by a stubborn and fiery temperament.

It is also interesting as I have seen alternate spellings with a second N, which would make this a 1, showing the power of the names.

Ines with her five-ruled name, who has a personality of Five, needs to remember to take breaks. Fives are going all the time, perhaps a frequenter of shows and concerts, so downtime can be important in this case.

It is always worth leaning into the things that make you happy, but balance is incredibly important.

Six

Six is a feminine number that aligns with the planet Venus. It holds the letters U, V, and W.

Six is parental, a nurturing and loving number, often seen to be the caring one since this number signifies compassion and wanting to put others first. The number being parental is important because it shows that some aspects are physical needs, not just ideals.

However, one of the many pitfalls is that the nurturing aspects can become overbearing, even appearing as an arrogance born of self-righteousness.

Example Name: Dean, 4+5+1+5=15, 1+5=6

Interestingly, the term self-righteous comes up when we consider that a dean is also the term for a scholarly position. I jest, of course, but an interesting tidbit.

If your name is Dean and your personality number is 6, chances are you will make a great dad or father figure. Mentoring might be something that suits your energy, again feeding into that scholarly note I raised.

Seven

Sevens cover the letters O and Z and fall under Neptune. They have a feminine energy. Sevens are our thinkers, our analysts, and our statisticians; they are the ones who look at the world through a logical lens.

While they can be spiritual, they have a hard time grasping religious ideals as they think about our world and the energies in it. They are often seen as philosophers. Music often speaks to Sevens, where they resonate with the meaning of it on a spiritual level.

Example Name: Luke, 3+6+2+5=16, 1+6=7

What we see in people with the digit sum 7 against their name is the capacity to think about the grander world. While this can leave them appearing disinterested, the opposite is true; Sevens are thinkers rather than doers.

For Sevens, I would always advise that they find new ideas to analyze, to feed that inner drive to know and understand, and to go out and take on the questions in the everyday. Where do fairytales come from? Why do certain sayings exist? Questions and answers help Sevens flourish.

Eight

Eight contains the letters F and P, and this is the number representative of the infinite, the unending. Eight is ruled by the planet Saturn, with the ring thought to be a representation of the unending as it loops around this celestial body infinitely.

Eight is the energy you look up to, a figure of authority. They have quiet endurance as a strength, pushing themselves and others to succeed with their empathic drive.

However, this drive and authority can lead to frustration born of things not being good enough. This satisfaction can grow into aggression, and this is something that Eights need to be careful of.

Example Name: Stephen, 3+4+5+8+5+5+5=35, 3+5=8

This is another example of where adopting a different name can lead to different energy. Where a Stephen is an 8, Steve would be a 5, and Steven a 1.

Stephens who have a personality number that complements their name's energy will be focused, and this is both a good thing and a bad thing as the emphasis on the focus can mean that they miss the opportunity to relax or learn.

Holding meetings for brainstorming will allow our friend Stephen to have a grasp on the leadership elements they have and to open up their way of thinking to the ideas of others.

Nine

While this number doesn't rule any letters, it is still part of our conversation as it influences names.

Nine is a masculine energy and is ruled by Mars; however, unlike the mythological god of war, this energy is humane, creative, and considerate of the world and the people around it. It shows compassion.

Example Name: Paul, 8+1+6+3=18, 1+8=9

Kind and considerate, Pauls put others first and are the ones we confide in.

They could benefit from putting themselves first occasionally. Removing themselves from toxic situations can be hard for a Nine, and this is especially true if their personality number is a match.

Famous Examples

For our famous Five, we look at the names Neil and Neal, as both come to a 5. Neal Smith is the drummer of the rock band Alice

Cooper, and Neil Gaiman is the author of books like *Good Omens* and *American Gods*.

While these examples are different people, we know that Fives are free-willed and driven, things you need in both disciplines.

Dean Cain, the actor who portrayed Superman in *The Adventures of Lois and Clark* TV series, is both our example of a Dean and a famous Six, and while this number doesn't speak much for his creativity in his roles, his caring side always carries a sincerity that would maybe be more difficult were he not a Six.

Luke is a Seven, a number that is focused on the grander world, and this number also has a connection to music and the feelings it provides.

We need look no further than Luke Bryan, a famous country singer. What is interesting about this Luke is that it is his stage name. Perhaps he felt that musical connection in his soul?

Stephen Hawking is our Eight, embodying the drive to succeed and the quiet reassurance and knowledge of the infinite we see in Eights. He is easily the clearest embodiment of this philosophy that I could show you.

Famous Nines are last, and perhaps the most famous is Paul McCartney, one of the Beatles, and a legend in his own right. He shows elements of creativity and humanity that we associate with the number 9, which sits nicely within what we know of Sir Paul.

When Names Are Changed

Many great performers have adopted a stage name. Writers like J.K. Rowling and E.L. James have adopted pen names, and while this is done for several reasons, these are just a couple of examples of a name that has changed.

Changing your name is a symbol or act of control. It is a change in the narrative of the individual and their energies. But why does this happen, and is this something you should consider?

While a stage name and pen name are a great tool for many artists, such as Banksy, who can use this name to protect their real life and to avoid the burden of fame or infamy, the need for one is a complex decision.

When asking yourself if you should change your name, the answer should be yes if it serves you a purpose that feels right and no if you feel much more comfortable with the name you have now and the energy that it provides you.

Many people are successful without a stage or pen name, so it is entirely situational with the needs of the individual being the crux. This is not a question I can answer specifically for you, but once we have discussed the reasons these things happen, you can better make that decision.

Pen Names and Stage Names

A pen name, otherwise known as a nom de plume, is the name adopted by a writer under which to publish work that may be outside of their usual genre, and a stage name is the same for a singer, musician, or actor.

Names like these are generally temporary names developed as a persona that is portrayed to the public. This is a character, a form of self that the individual behind the name is broadcasting. This name is often used to replace their name to reap benefits from the things they perceive the pseudonym can provide.

In the example of musicians, it could be that the name has a better sound to it, like Elton John compared to Reginald Dwight or Lady Gaga compared to Stefani Germanotta. Their given names and their stage names are different in the structural sense, but they also provide the reader of those names with a different energy.

With some bands from Scandinavia, stage names are part of the presentation. In the genre of music known as black metal, many of the performers wear face paint, costumes, and have character names, thus allowing them a sense of creative freedom and personal distancing from their daily lives.

Some pen names, such as the aforementioned J.K. Rowling and E.L. James, are adopted to take on more gender-neutral or masculine tones with the belief being that this would allow for better sales and coverage of the product. Whether this works is up for debate, but that is the reasoning behind that particular change.

Changing a Name Legally

The other side of the discussion is far more complex—the act of legally changing a name. There are a great many reasons for someone to want or need to change their name legally. This could be due to a family reason or a desire to distance themselves from their family.

It could be caused by marriage or divorce or a desire to take on the name you have used as a stage name as your real name.

But the biggest part of this consideration is the soul. Sometimes, people are born in the wrong body, a male soul in a female body or a female soul in a male body, and this person realizes they identify as the gender of their soul. They see that the energy of their name is part of the trappings they were incorrectly born with, and they find a trueness in their new name, their new identity.

They will pick a name they are drawn to or that they like and embrace this new personality by finally embracing the fullest truth of who they are and correcting the wrongness of the energy they previously felt.

There is also the act of a company changing its name or the name of a product being changed. This could be due to several factors; the most famous one that springs to my mind is the change of the WWF.

In the early stages of the new millennium, the World Wildlife Fund and the World Wrestling Federation had several court meetings to discuss the issue of both companies being known as the WWF.

The World Wrestling Federation eventually changed its name to World Wrestling Entertainment, and its abbreviation became WWE.

While there are likely countless examples of this, it just goes to show that even large companies can have disputes due to the value of a name.

Nicknames

Nicknames, sometimes referred to as pet names, are things we attribute to individuals around us, be they born of playfulness, because the person reminds us of a character or celebrity, or because we always see them under certain circumstances.

Nicknames are a term of endearment and can lend to that individual different energies and vibrations than their given name provides.

Some nicknames are derived from the person's actual name and can carry similar kinds of energy while also allowing that person to feel and be a little bit different.

Nicknames are the person-to-person equivalent of a stage name or pen name in that they are not a permanent shift in identity or energy; instead, they are a temporary transference of these vibrations.

The Ruling Planets

Throughout our journey, we have made references to planets ruling over the numbers, but what does it mean when we talk about which numbers and letters sit with or, more precisely, are ruled by each of the celestial bodies?

What this means is that the planets, the Moon, and the Sun govern energy that affects us on a spiritual level. They guide us and change our vibrations and the vibrations of those around us. They can help us to see the grander pattern not just in the day to day but also in ourselves.

They can help us plan, change, and grow. They can guide us to better results, while also showing us when to wait for a moment that better suits our needs.

They share their names with the gods of old religions, and maybe there is a reason behind this. Perhaps the deities of that time are connected to us through energy.

Ascendant

When we say that a planet is in ascension or an ascendant phase, this means it is in an upward, rising motion. This complements its usual energy and vibration, strengthening the influence it has. It can be caused by the motion of this planet or by a retrograde motion elsewhere in the cosmos.

Where the planet is emotional or intellectual, these traits become enlightened, allowing for those affected by the change to be more receptive than they usually would be. This may be why we feel unexplained moments of joy and calm or moments of pure inspiration.

We can see that on these days and in these weeks, our energy changes, and we must learn to track and look into the movements of our governing celestial body to better understand what we are feeling and how best to capitalize on it.

This can be done, much like a horoscope, through a numeroscope, which we discussed in Chapter 1. We can begin to see the right times to start something new or know when our energies are more likely to thrive.

But what happens when the opposite is true? What happens when these truths are flipped?

Retrograde

When we say that a planet is in retrograde, it doesn't always mean down, although there is a downward element to it. Retrograde means to go in reverse, to shift the paradigm. This can lead to some interesting side effects.

Most notably, the vibrations and energies we feel under normal circumstances are reversed or disrupted at the least, meaning that we may begin to struggle with our emotions or logic, or our drive may feel like it is struggling to engage.

This can lead to feelings of lethargy and disheartened unease. Depression is common in retrograde for more emotive numbers, so this is something we need to look at more closely.

When we begin to study and look into this, we can better plan how we prepare for these changes in both our energies and the energies of those around us.

Where our numeroscope can tell us of the potential for good, it can also forewarn us of the potential disruption by a ruling planet in retrograde, allowing us to prepare ourselves accordingly.

Under the most normal of circumstances, planets and their energies will travel from east to west in the night sky; however, planets can appear to reverse this journey through their shifting alignment with the stars.

This gives the impression of a backward or retrograde motion, which was noted in many ancient cultures as an omen and is the basis of how we measure the ruling planets' effects on us.

Numbers and the Divine

It is no accident that the worlds of astrology and numerology share a lot of commonalities. It is also not surprising that elements of many religions and spirituality share these common threads.

A big part of the human experience is to try and make sense of the greater mysteries of our existence and our place in the cosmos.

We see continued threads of the messages we can derive from the stars and the weight of destiny on each person. We also see that people do struggle in pursuit of these teachings.

A lot of what we now consider pagan beliefs focused on gods that were representative of the planets. Many modern beliefs have these ruled by concepts with the Sun itself being representative of many more widely worshiped principal deities.

We see these connections between the worship of the planets and gods and the subsequent relationship between the planets, numbers, and us. It is all in the same vein, where these energies influence and guide us, teach and warn us. Numbers can seem divine, and divinity can be seen as celestial energy.

What Have We Learned?

In this stage of our journey, we learned the power of our names and began to look at the lessons they provide us with the emphasis now becoming much more focused on the intricate parts of who we are and what those things translate to.

We can see the coming together of a personality number and the numbers we can divine from our names and how, if these match, they can make us prone to the core elements of those numbers and our ruling celestials.

But what do we do if we have multiple elements? How do we balance conflicting numbers? We do this in much the same way we balance everything. We find a compromise, as we have already discussed, by identifying the negative aspects of the influences in ourselves and how to manage them.

We have also learned that changing names can change the energy they present, and this is why some people identify as a different name, even if they perhaps don't realize it. They are likely reacting to the vibrations of a name that doesn't quite feel right.

We have learned that there are many reasons why someone may change their name and adopt a persona for themselves, and this is influenced by how that new name makes them feel and how it vibrates with their energies.

The End of Chapter Deep Dive

The next deep dive I want to discuss is currently subject to a bit of debate because some think that every conversation we have is recorded. I am sure you have probably heard this one before, but let me ask all the same: Have you ever seen an advertisement on Facebook, Twitter, Instagram, or any of the millions of websites out there?

Chances are that yes, you have, but did you know that a lot of math and, therefore, numbers go into those advertisements? Were you aware that information stored about you in the form of 'cookies' feeds this math?

The truth is that to many corporations in this world, all people are little more than the statistics they represent, and as such, there are equations and demographics they identify among the populace. While this is a slightly unsatisfying idea, it is interesting for several reasons. This is because they primarily identify people based on the idea of their age, gender, where they are from, and the people in their social circles.

This is why it will sometimes feel like social media and our devices are listening to us all of the time. We may well be discussing things we like or want to do when seemingly from nowhere, an advertisement for that thing or something incredibly similar will crop up.

The truth is that websites and social media use complex forms of math to determine the things you are likely to like based on the aforementioned factors, and they pair it with the information they have access to from cookies, creating a likelihood ratio, best shown in a Venn diagram.

A Venn diagram is the visual representation of a form of logical thinking. It may show that people who like dinosaurs and are in their 30s have likely got a dinosaur mug. This kind of logical thinking starts with numbers and applies to the lessons we are learning.

If you have the personality numbers 4 and 7 and your name has the value of 4, your 4 becomes dominant. This can determine factors about you using similar logical thinking. Are you more likely to prefer leading or following? Are you likely to enjoy creating content or consuming it?

We know this kind of logical thinking exists in Boolean Logic—a form of algebra—where we make statements around the 'if' and 'then' logic. For example, if someone likes dinosaurs, then this person probably wants a dinosaur mug.

If we can accept that the algorithm of Facebook can tell us that we want to buy a dinosaur mug, can't we accept that the algorithm of our universe tells us that we need more time to meditate?

Chapter 6:

Making Numbers Work for You

We have covered a lot of ground together so far, but to truly grasp the concepts of numerology in relation to the self, even now that we have a better understanding of ourselves, our energies, and the universe around us, we need to start looking at the things we can be doing to help make those energies and vibrations work for us.

In this stage of our journey together, we will start to unfold our knowledge into practical applications. We will look at how we can create energies based on the timing of a project and even the names we give to something.

We will look at the good and bad of timing and how vibrations affect us and ask ourselves tough questions relating to our sought-after goals and aspirations.

Once we have, we will see that we can influence the universe with positive energy just by planning and putting the numbers to work for us and that we can start to benefit from the energies we get back in return.

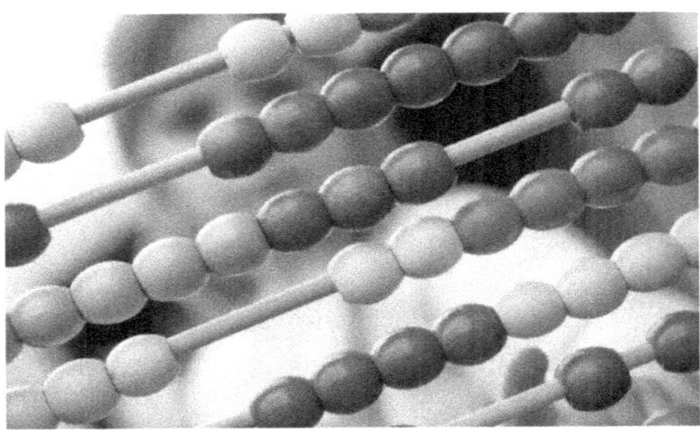

Identifying the Opportunity

In life, few opportunities are telegraphed with neon signs, so we need to try and spot them ourselves. Opportunities are like anything in life; we know and understand what they are and where they come from, but we don't always know how to recognize them in advance. But that is where this stage of our journey takes us, to a mindset where we can begin to identify something ahead of time.

Take, for example, the notion of supply and demand, which is an economic concept that identifies a demand for a product or service in the world and decides how to supply and profit from it. Consider that sales of umbrellas often increase in wetter months or that products like road salt are less widely purchased in summer months.

Now, this may all sound cynical, but the fact is that not all opportunities are purely financially driven. Some are driven purely by the creative or caring part of the soul, where we have a spiritual need to act to benefit us or those around us. Therefore, there are opportunities to do something from a non-commercial standpoint.

This benefit is, in fact, where we start to look at our opportunity. It could be a product that would help us or a story we are longing to tell or a way we are looking to help someone we care about. It could be a song we want to sing or a room we realize could be rearranged to allow for a more comfortable seating plan.

This is our opportunity, and once we have identified it, we need to start looking at when the right moment is and, conversely, when to wait.

Knowing the Right Time to Act

Sometimes, a project will come along, and it just resonates with the soul. This is the first and clearest indication that a project or opportunity has come along at the right time. When you can feel it, it is often referred to as a eureka or lightbulb moment.

But this isn't the only factor that can tell us if it is the right time. For example, you may begin to work on a project and realize that while this is something you want to see to completion, it is not something you want to put out into the world. You'll also know when the opposite is true.

You may absentmindedly begin to do something for yourself and realize that this thing that you are undertaking is the opportunity and that you can begin to put the energy out there to see how it is received.

Generally, you'll know if an idea or opportunity is good by the reactions of people. Talk to your friends and loved ones about the project; discuss how they feel about it, the negatives and positives. They may or may not support the idea. There's an adage that no one likes everything, and knowing that a good opportunity may not apply to everyone is a great skill to have.

If an idea comes to you when your ruling planet is in ascension, this is a project you should jump on.

How the project makes you feel is also worth keeping in mind. If the energy you have when working on the project is positive, then the time is now to work toward your goal, whatever that may be, as this positive feeling is the vibrations of the cosmos in you and your soul.

Knowing the Wrong Time to Act

For every successful project, there are those projects that don't work. There are canceled movies, games, and TV shows. There are hundreds of examples we could use from many forms of media, and the same is true at a personal level.

When we start a project, it may at first feel like the right thing, but that may change. As I previously mentioned, the act of stopping is not only natural, but it is also good for the soul. Sometimes, a project may be one you simply realize isn't resonating with you anymore, and it is okay to walk away.

For some of the more stubborn and headstrong numbers, walking away from projects is always going to be the biggest hurdle to overcome.

Projects can fall by the wayside for several reasons. Maybe the project was taking too long, the learning curve was too steep, or it wasn't vibrating the way you had hoped. These all sound like excuses, but the truth is that this is your soul telling you this is the time to stop.

That doesn't mean you will never finish the project. You may later find a flash of inspiration, a call to arms as it were, where you return to it when the time is right.

If your ruling celestial body is in retrograde, this is a good time to put a project on the back burner because you may grow frustrated. Since your energy will be out of sorts, this makes sense, so put things on hold until you begin to feel more like yourself.

The other thing to consider is if you are working on a goal for yourself or others. If you are working on something that is for or with others, it could be a good idea to turn to them for help and inspiration, especially if your energy levels are dwindling. If they advise you to put it aside, then you can always do so, but you never know where you might find help.

Planning and Execution

"When you fail to plan, you plan to fail."

I cannot express how many times I have heard this saying and how true it can be. Not knowing a route can leave you lost, and not knowing the skills required can lead to some embarrassing side effects.

For as much as heading into a project can be determined by when it feels right, there are other aspects of the project to consider. Take the example of getting fit. The core ideas are to lose weight and exercise, and you may feel the time is right. But what are the best methods?

Here, we will be discussing good planning practices, showing you how to begin to structure your ideas and goals to make them more attainable, more achievable.

When we plan, we can start to put our knowledge of the universe to use, and progress is a process, as they say.

I will say before we start that even with the best of intentions, things can go awry. There are unforeseen complications and unknown influences. A lot can and will go wrong, but don't worry. We cover what to do if it all comes apart.

Good Planning Techniques

The first step in any plan, regardless of the scale of the end goal, is a little research. If you want to lose weight, look up tips and tricks. If you want to learn to swim, look for classes. Research of your intended end goal is the best place to start. This will help you in several ways, especially when planning around beneficial energies.

When we research things, the best thing to do is to keep notes purely because we can go back to our notes later. Note that this may not seem pertinent for all objectives, but the truth is that developing research as a habit is a great skill to have.

The second step would be to set an initial goal. This is a small goal based on your research. Let's use the example that you want to learn to paint. You've researched local classes and found one that suits your needs. Now, you have to set your first goal; it could be to buy some pencils or paper or even just to attend the class itself.

Your first goal should always be something attainable. In regards to painting, becoming an overnight Picasso is unlikely. Setting goals that we fail at can be demoralizing, which is why research is so important. We can see the experiences of others, both those who have succeeded and those who have failed, and draw interesting lessons in all respects.

The third step is to start setting time for the betterment of this task. Sticking with painting, the classes are great, but if you are only painting once a week or even once a month, progress will be slow, which, like setting the initial bar too high, can be demoralizing.

The best course is always to set aside extra time to practice, even if it is just small bursts twice a week. "Little and often" is a great learning mindset and can help you form good habits.

This is especially true if you are a beginner. There is a reason many disciplines, from art to health and fitness, have beginner classes. The idea of starting something and instantly being a master at it is unlikely.

Our fourth step is to seek out like-minded people. Look for social groups of people doing or learning to do the thing you are doing, and while being cautious to not compete, look to them for inspiration, going at a comfortable pace.

Having like-minded peers is a great resource, both for positive energy and for finding out what works and what doesn't. We can share our disappointments safely and constructively, and without realizing it, we could be both teaching and learning from these mistakes.

Asking the Tough Questions

There will be times during the planning and execution of projects that we have to ask ourselves tough questions. This is an unavoidable part of the human experience and should be embraced.

We ask ourselves these questions as a way of making sense of our experience. Take, for example, the question, do I have time? With this question, we are looking to see if the extra exertion and pressure is worthwhile.

This feeds back into the idea of our energies and our vibrations as affected by our ruling celestial bodies. We can review if we need to take a break or adjust how we are doing the project based on if these bodies are in ascension or retrograde.

For example, we may be asking ourselves if we have time because we may not feel it is presently the right time to undertake our project. We may also be feeling that we have not prepared enough, so when we are asking ourselves if we can do something, the reasons we are asking need to be considered.

One of the toughest questions will come when we fail. Failure is a natural part of life and is a truth many people shy away from; however, we always need to ask ourselves why we failed.

There are countless experiences I could relate to you here. Edison inventing the light bulb, J.K. Rowling and Harry Potter's success—all are a testament to how we fail but grow.

Once we ask why, we can look at what we can learn, what we can do better, and what new ideas we can try. Failing is one of the most important aspects of succeeding, and asking the question "what went wrong?" is as important as our research.

We also need to start to be aware of how the project is affecting our energies and how that is affecting the people around us. This consideration is so that we reflect on how the project or objective is making us feel. If we feel tired and stressed due to the thing we are doing, perhaps it is time to ask if we should take a break.

When It Goes Wrong Anyway

Part of life is falling down, but to quote an oft-quoted phrase, it is not how many times you get knocked down but how many times you get back up that matters.

There will be times where everything you put together looks great, every plan and procedure is in place, and you have taken every learning opportunity you can to close any foreseen gaps you have in your knowledge base. You go about the preparation with the best of intentions, and all the energy you have is aligned.

And then, like a house of cards, it tumbles down. It can and does happen, and this is when that attitude of getting back on the horse comes into play. The worst thing you can do with failure is to let it drag you down. As much as good energy can breed more good energy, bad energy will often lead to more bad energy.

Good Vibrations

Throughout our journey, we have discussed vibrations a bit, and I wanted to discuss vibrations a bit more. We know now that each person has vibrations determined by their name, their day and year of birth, as well as their ruling celestial body.

When all of these things are in harmony, we experience good vibrations, and the very fibers of our souls come alive, moments of epiphany like clarity in our lives.

These vibrations are to be savored and enjoyed. We can use them to broaden our effectiveness in the cosmos by breathing in the very air around us and allowing our positivity to shine.

There is a reason that music talks to us. We know music is vibrations and numbers, so music that appeals to us speaks to our soul. We, in the same way, can project our positivity onto others with our vibrations.

The ascension and retrograde of planets can affect our energy, so forming the habit of consulting a numeroscope can begin to better inform us of why we may be feeling out of sorts with ourselves.

Repeating Numbers

In life, we will see repeating numbers. I just wanted to talk a little as to why that is and what we can do to either encourage or avoid it, should we so wish to do so.

In the Jim Carrey movie *The Number 23*, the protagonist starts seeing the number 23 in everything, from his social security number to addresses. While I won't spoil the plot here, it is interesting that the film acknowledges the patterns of numbers we have in the everyday.

Number patterns are codes, meanings, messages, and warnings. The trick is to take the time to listen to the messages we are receiving from those numbers or from the dates that matter to us that we see in other places, like a date important to us referred to in a TV show.

There are people whose specialty is code-breaking, working out the complex, seemingly random codes and patterns, using what is called a cipher. Once identified, the cipher is the key for the pattern or code, and once we have it, the code begins to make sense, which is why numerology talks a lot about the cosmic patterns in our lives.

Patterns can speak to us. One of the more interesting ones is seeing digital clocks with the same numbers across the whole display, 11:11 or 5:55 for example. If you find yourself noticing these numbers all of the time, there is likely a message you need to receive.

The writer Sergei Lukyanenko has this as a minor plot point in his *Night Watch* books, where if someone sees these repeating numbers, they are more in tune with magic. I find this worth mentioning because it is in an interesting parallel to the real energies of numerology.

When we are seeing repeating numbers, there is an underlying code, a reason. It is a message of sorts, and we need to start trying to decipher this code, take our key and cipher, and answer these messages.

The truth is that this message and these numbers will be different for each of us who experience them, but reflecting on how they make us feel can give us keys, and that is our first step.

What Have We Learned?

In this chapter, we have learned what an opportunity is and how to spot it. We have learned that there is a good time to approach a project or opportunity, and looking at the factors that can point us in the right direction can enlighten our decision.

We have learned that sometimes, it is okay and in our best interests to put a project or goal on hold because the energies we draw may become out of sync. We can always return to a project if we need to.

We have learned how to make a plan, how to execute said plan, and how to ask ourselves the tough questions we need to ask whenever we come to a difficult time in anything we are trying to achieve.

We have looked specifically at good vibrations and how best to capitalize on them to draw the best energies and, in turn, the best results from ourselves.

And, with a little help from a movie, we have drawn some understanding of the messages we can learn from repeating numbers.

The End of Chapter Deep Dive

A haiku is a poem written in a structure based around the moras of words. While there is no direct translation for moras, in the Western world, we use syllables, meaning that the poem has a structure based on its rhythm. While many rhyming poems take on rhythmic structures, referred to as stanzas, it is interesting to know a structure like this exists as a rule.

Language and structure can be seen as numbers. Our voices carry vibrations in how we convey a word or emotive sound, and in poetry, this is pronounced. When reading a poem, the rhythm and structure of the poem often lead to the reader taking on a more somber or joyous cadence depending on the energy transcribed into the way the poem is written.

This is even true of the way fiction and non-fiction works are read. If you listen to audiobooks, the voice is kept in an informal, friendly tone as that is generally the way that the material was written.

However, when the structure of a fact

Is molded to something poetic,

We don't know how to act.

The voice becomes slightly artistic.

Did you feel that? The change in how the information was presented changed the tone you read my voice in, and all of that was achieved by understanding the rhythm and patterns of numbers in our speech.

This happens in language and songs specifically more than you think. A change in the vibration of a note or the cadence of the singer is more likely to draw an emotional response from us, and much like that change in writing style may inform the tone of how it is read, the same is true of the music.

Another interesting phenomenon in the written word I wanted to touch on to show you just how interlinked music and vibrations and words are is onomatopoeia. This is the use of words that remind you of sounds or words that are the sounds being used for the effect of creating the sound. Examples include beep, boom, or meow.

This is even more profound when paired with alliteration, the act of using repeating word sounds to emphasize a sound.

This shows that how we change the energy and cadence of something can change how this is interpreted and how it affects those who experience it, much like our vibrations.

Chapter 7:

Inner Chaos

The opposite of order is chaos. Chaos can be thought of as a storm, a whirling cyclone of destructive power. It is disruptive energy that will affect us all.

Some days, we wake up and the sky is clear and blue, yet the world around us is at odds with how we feel. Our inner self is in flux, and we feel adrift, lost in a storm cloud at sea.

We've all been there, spilled coffee, forgotten our phone, or stubbed our collective toes on every door frame imaginable. Maybe we left the oven on, set off the fire alarm, found our cat stuck in a tree, or snapped the handle off of our favorite cup before a sip could be taken.

While these things are all physical, they branch from something that is happening to us in the vibrations of the world. You see, there are several factors that can lead to us feeling overwhelmed spiritually, leading to moments where it begins to feel like the universe has turned against us. It is here that we will begin to discuss, address, and fix this feeling.

We will look at our inner chaos and identify the issues causing it so that each time these feelings of unease or trepidation arise, we can begin to understand them and deal with them healthily and constructively.

This means that in the future, we will know when to have a lid on our coffees, when to wear steel-toed slippers around the house, and when to buy a ladder to rescue the cat ourselves.

What Creates Chaos?

As always, our next step in understanding the thing we need to address is to ask the right questions, even if the answer seems large and unwieldy. So, let us ask ourselves, what is chaos?

Chaos is like a disharmonious noise. It is an overabundance of energies crashing like waves on the sea. We can see chaos in times of uncertainty or when there is a rush to get something done by people who are not prepared for it or are too tired to think. It is an overabundance of traffic with blaring horns and information leading to a crescendo that our souls cannot compute.

But more specifically, we have to ask, what creates a chaos of the soul? This imbalance is not only normal, but it is also something that can be caused by internal or external factors.

Chaos can be born of uncertainty, fear, anger, and sadness. All of these emotions can and do create chaos inside of us. These may be from factors that we cannot control, such as pain or loss, but often, there are factors that we can influence both in ourselves and our outer influences.

Noise is a good example. If you are exposed to the pounding noise of construction and car horns honking for a long period, it can lead to distress and feed the chaos inside of you.

If you take the example of noise a step further, then chaos is standing in a busy terminal of a train station. Everyone is talking with excessively loud music and children crying. The layer upon layer becomes a cacophony, and we struggle to tune it out. Even reading those sentences may make you feel uncomfortable, and that is what chaos is.

But how do we remove these feelings? How do we control chaos as best as possible? In this stage of our journey, we will begin to tackle this discomfort head-on because if we can calm the chaos, it is one less hurdle to clear.

Creating Rituals

In this section, we will be looking at the benefits of routine and rituals. When I say rituals, don't worry; there will be no violence toward animals or summoning involved. There's far too much to clean up after.

We are more concerned with living through chaos than trying to ignore it. You see, dear reader, chaos is, by its definition, the lack or loss of order. While it might seem like chaos may suit some numbers, the truth is that even those who rebel only do so because they perceive chaos and endeavor to change it to a fairer order.

Chaos is never something that is actively sought out, at least not by anyone outside of the science community, where the understanding of chaos is a core pursuit.

Creating a controllable order can help to remove feelings of chaos from the soul. This is where rituals come in. Rituals don't have to be complex; they can range from making an 11 am coffee to watching your favorite show at 5 pm.

Rituals can also mean how we prepare. Maybe you get up at 6:30 am, shower, brush your teeth, make a coffee, and eat breakfast. This makes up your morning routine or ritual. You are used to it, but maybe you need to add a walk to your morning routine to allow your energy to disperse. Changes like these can help you immensely.

Rituals and routines are the act of repetition to create order, which can help to assuage chaos.

Little Rituals to Try

It can be difficult at first to create new rituals, so I wanted to make some suggestions for you. These are not based on your number or anything like that since these three little rituals can apply to all numbers. Since you don't have to try all three, it allows you to pick one and see if it works. That way, you are not trying too many things at once.

So, my first one is to replace music with podcasts one day a week. If you listen to music in the car, oftentimes, those tunes can start to grate on you, so set aside one day where, via the magic that is Bluetooth, you connect your phone to your car and play a pre-downloaded podcast of your choice.

Even if you don't have a car, this is still a great thing to try by listening at home. Replacing TV for a day can give you a different take, breaking up your week.

This can also help you to learn things regarding the project or process you are working through, giving you experience outside of your own.

The second thing to try is collecting things. This could be stickers, fridge magnets, dolls, plush toys, or even baseball cards. Collecting is something that we all do anyway, but replacing the collection we have of internalized fatigue with something that makes us smile is crucial.

You can even replace the idea of collecting physical things with collecting photographs. Take photos you think are beautiful or strange. This gives you something else to focus on instead of the everyday grind.

This collection can be looked at in times when there is too much noise or chaos, allowing your mind to focus on something pleasing, dispelling the negativity in a real way.

The third thing anyone could try is setting alarms. The reason so many of us feel tired is that we never program our body clocks the correct way. We need alarms set every morning and a clear bedtime to get enough sleep. Creating a routine is important to our souls, even if we are rebellious.

You'll be able to tell how sleep is affecting you by considering how long you sleep without an alarm. This is why reprogramming yourself is super important, and having device time minimized in the buildup to bedtime can help.

One final routine to try is setting small targets. A word count for work, an improvement in how fast you do something, how much water you drink in a day—these habits and rituals are more important than I can express and are something you should invest time into.

Decluttering

Go to the nearest drawer, cupboard, or shelf in your household and look at all of the objects. Try to remember where and when you got each one. It may be a lot harder than you think.

Over time, we accumulate a lot of stuff, both in the physical, real sense and in the metaphysical, spiritual sense. The idea of decluttering feeds back into the idea of clearing out our energy. That ritual walk you may have added to your weekly routine can also be part of the declutter because it can serve as a time to evaluate.

Things you hold on to, both physically and emotionally, can be bad for you, and as such, making the choice to tidy those away is important and will ultimately help you create positive vibrations.

Think of your mind like a garage where you store all the tools and materials you've ever needed with all the skills and knowledge packed in boxes. Unsurprisingly, over time, the boxes and baggage you collect begin to clutter that garage, making it difficult for you to maneuver around, making being in that space undesirable and uncomfortable.

This is true both of your actual garage and the garage in your mind, so remember to discard negative and toxic clutter as often as you can. This is especially true for remnants of old relationships or old friendships. Relationships that have burned out can leave a stain on us if we let them; removing items pertaining to those times is always a good plan.

I touched on collecting in rituals, and I think that is true, but keeping those things in a specific place is also important. Like books on a shelf or dishes in a rack, everything having its place is a part of the decluttering process and is something we can practice in all aspects of ourselves.

Decluttering doesn't strictly mean throwing out all the old stuff you have. That is part of it, sure, but it could also simply mean organizing our clutter into a new configuration. One of the best tips could simply be to buy a few large plastic tubs and store old stuff in those.

Moving stuff from cardboard boxes to plastic tubs is a good decluttering exercise because we can question our attachment to and the value of each item as we move it. We can discard items as we go along.

Once we have embraced this, we can use decluttering as a ritual, further expanding our control over the self and the physical. Making it a quarterly exercise is more than enough. Most people who embrace this method of sorting do it once a year, thus the term spring-cleaning.

Another great thing to try is to rearrange furniture. Our homes are the space we spend our downtime in. These spaces should feel free, calm, and welcoming. Think of how stressful moving is and how satisfying it feels when we finally reach a status quo of order.

Over time, that fresh move-in feel begins to collect clutter and feel at odds. Refreshing that feeling by organizing or even flipping a room's layout is a breath of fresh air to our souls.

Make Space for Happiness

In the act of decluttering and creating rituals, we have begun to make room in our lives, and that room should be for happiness.

The modern world is fast-paced and always on the move. We can often become caught up in the tide of life, and we don't always stop to make time for the things that make us happy.

In our routines, when planning projects, and in everything we do, we still need to set aside some time and say to ourselves, "This is when I am doing what makes me happy." Everything doesn't have to be about work or our projects or anyone else if we don't want it to be.

This does need to be something we love to do, be it reading a book, watching a movie, or having a little "me time" in a hot bath with a glass of wine. Whatever is your chicken soup for the soul, do it, and make time for it.

What Makes Us Happy?

Happiness is a science. I know it is weird to think of it that way, but it is true. Things that vibrate with us the right way and bring us happiness are the things that trigger reactions in our brains. Now, for you and me, this may be different, but that is the point, is it not?

One of the phrases that have always somewhat perplexed me is the phrase "guilty pleasure," which implies that you like this thing but should be ashamed of it. Happiness should never be embarrassing; it should be celebrated.

There is a community of people out there who love your guilty pleasure, and if there isn't, perhaps you could form that community page.

Happiness is the triggering of joy through a reaction of the brain to the energy of the self. It is the hairs that stand up during the beautiful song or epic scene. Please embrace it, dear reader.

It could be reading a good book or watching a B movie. It could be playing video games or drinking a glass of red wine while watching something on a streaming service. Whatever makes your brain satisfied needs to be repeated where possible.

Because, if we start denying ourselves relaxation and fun, we begin to mentally clutter ourselves with fatigue and dissatisfaction.

Aside from the things that make us happy, there are other things we need to make space for, like our projects and opportunities. I just wanted to give a few tips to keep in mind for making space for this.

If you are planning to take up running, buy a specific pair of running shoes for that activity and store them in a specific bag. If you are planning to write, draw, or photograph, have a special desk or area where you can practice this thing that you are yearning for.

If you are looking to learn to cook, setting aside time in the kitchen for yourself could be vital. Having physical space for the passion you have come to pursue will be of the utmost importance.

If space in your home is limited, the idea of social groups and group spaces is your next best option.

You must find the space for your projects and passions, even if that space is a little hard to come by at first, because this will create a discipline, an association, that you go there to do that specifically, allowing your brain to switch to that mode.

Understanding the Blueprint for Life

Much like a church or a skyscraper, some plans relate to who you are. From the moment we are born and choose our true name, our soul has a blueprint laid out for us.

Now that we have begun to see which numbers define us, we should start seeing elements of ourselves in our numbers and in the digit sums that show who we are. We need to start understanding that the same is true of all things and all people.

We need to learn to trust our intuition and our blueprint so that we can truly begin to maximize our lives, embracing the things we can control, making the most of the energies we receive from the cosmos.

While our blueprints are different, we are all on our journeys together, so helping and encouraging each other is incredibly important.

This blueprint is our destiny, but how do we begin to determine what we are being told by our energies? How do we read this blueprint?

What Is the Blueprint?

When we discuss the blueprint, we are talking about something incredibly personal that, much like the idea of star signs, is indicative of a potential rather than a guarantee. For example, we may have aspects that indicate a creative side, but we do not find ourselves drawn to that aspect.

This could be due to cosmic clues, but first, let us try to understand what happens if aspects of our numbers are drawing us in. These include elements of our name, personality, the days we feel inspired, and the patterns we have been seeing throughout.

If your name and your personality numbers are both showing a creative, caring element, and you are drawn to arts and expression but are not satisfied, it is likely caused by a lack of participation. The simple joy of watching or absorbing this art is no longer enough for you, so you now need to do it yourself.

You see, the "blueprint for life" is our call to arms at this moment; it is the energy we have been receiving, the feeling of being drawn to certain people, certain activities, or ways of thinking. These are messages that are determined for us by our ruling planets and our personality numbers. They are messages that we must be able to honestly assess and determine using what we know about who and where we are.

This is the cosmic plan for us, and all we do and can be is seen in the patterns around us. You may live in houses numbered 42, then 88, then 8. All of the numbers may be telling you something about your time in that place. They may want you to lead, or they may want you to create. Look at these numbers and see what digit sums they lead you to. What characteristics are associated with those?

This is the beginning of the blueprint that we can use to capitalize on our fullest potential. And when compared with all the other things we have learned, we come to learn that we are being drawn to paint for a living or to run a 10k or to record an album. Whatever the underlying end goal, we are gently being guided to it by the energies around us.

This is why we will feel a moment, a eureka moment as I called it previously, where something feels right. This is the universe and the blueprint itself letting you know that you are on the right path.

What Have We Learned?

In this stage of our journey, we have learned that rituals and routines are important to us, that decluttering can just mean tidying, and that removing negative clutter is good for all of us.

We learned that it is okay to love the things you love and that only you can make the time and space for the things that make you happy. Do not worry about guilty pleasures. If you find joy in them, they cannot be bad.

We also discussed the blueprint for life, what things we can draw from it, and how it can be seen in our numbers.

The End of Chapter Deep Dive

Did you know that the idea of chaos theory is that, even in seemingly random events, there is a pattern, a formula by which we can predict events? Under the seemingly random aspect of a disaster is a secret mathematical order to events.

Chaos theory is a scientific theory that speaks to the idea that everything is connected by energy and that we can predict events simply with numbers. It states that if scientists could crack this hidden code, they could unveil the mysteries of the world and all that is in it and prevent disasters before they could even happen.

Some films have chaos theory as a core plot element, such as the 2009 movie *Knowing* with Nicolas Cage as a man who ends up seeing the prediction of a series of events in a series of seemingly random numbers.

While the movie is fiction, the theory it draws inspiration from is one that is a real theory and enforces the beliefs of numerology.

But this isn't the only example of this kind of seemingly random pattern becoming something explainable. In the video game series Pokemon, players are tasked with venturing into the world and collecting the adorable titular creatures. In most games, the encounters seem random; however, there is math underneath the hood conjuring these creatures.

The same is true of a great many video games, where seemingly random incidents are generated by a preset series of numerical factors. The terms for this are "rogue-like" or "procedurally generated." The game will have preset factors and draw from these factors to shape the game as the player progresses, and while this will feel random, it is entirely marshaled by math and numbers. Maybe this is similar to our own blueprint?

Chapter 8:

Embracing the Numbers

Throughout this journey together, we have been learning the importance of numbers, the effect these have on our souls, and the things we can learn and reveal by seeing them for what they are.

This part of our journey is about accepting and embracing the truth of our numbers, of looking at ourselves as the various parts of our blueprint and accepting it.

We must learn to balance the leadership with the emotion, the chaos with the rational, and we must learn to do that by truly embracing the numbers in our lives. We must learn to be all that we can be by looking at the elements of our numbers and realizing that we always knew something, that some part of us was missing.

You may have been leading but still been deeply dissatisfied as you may not have been embracing your inner rebel, your inner creative. Only by leaning in and embracing the facts in our soul can we begin to fully understand who and what we are and who and what we were always meant to be.

This is about fulfilling our potential, seeing the dreams and aspirations we yearn for on a spiritual level, and aiming to achieve those with the skills we have already learned.

In this part of our journey together, we will be looking at how embracing the right numbers for a project or the right number for a price has helped established individuals garner success and how we can learn from those examples.

9s and 5s in Business

Business and numbers go hand in hand. This is neither surprising nor a new concept considering that the idea of trading began with the understanding that all things have an intrinsic value to us as human beings.

Any project can learn from the ideas of business. It is a staple of bringing the best out of a project or opportunity to look at what others did well, what they did badly, and what methods these people and businesses used in their decision-making processes.

We have talked about opportunities at some length, but this is a good thing to consider when looking at those opportunities. What are other people trying? What is working for them? What isn't working for them? It is worth noting that no idea is wholly original, so it is not what you do but how it is done that matters most.

When we look at how it is done in business, we can see that the numbers 9 and 5 are both incredibly important. If you were to go to a car dealership, you'll see many cars with a price ending in 9. The same is true in stores, both of prices ending in 9 or 5.

Think of any time you have seen a price ending in any other number, be it a 1 or a 7. It makes you feel uncomfortable. It seems strange or unsettling. That is an indicator of the influence of numbers and how they are ingrained within us.

The number 9 is finite, the end, but it also represents the compassion and humanity in us all, and so it makes us more drawn to the product. A product at $3.99 is more appealing than a product at $4, and that is because we are drawn to that 9.

Many businesses will launch products on days that have preferable numbers, such as the 23rd (5) or 27th (9) of the month. This is because, without us realizing it, we are drawn to those dates and, subsequently, those numbers.

Even the way stores stack and display their goods can be attributed to numbers. Prominent products are stored at heights more likely to catch the eye. Products can also often be displayed in groups, where too many or too few are seen as a negative. This is a business-level understanding of the balances we need to find in ourselves. Having the right balance of things is clearly key.

One of the most interesting numbers in business is also a theory that applies to us in the most pertinent way. It's called the economics of one unit, which is the practice of focusing on one product or one service at a time and then repeating to get that product or service perfect.

Similar to how we are learning to balance, we also need to learn to follow the following steps:

1. Take things one step at a time
2. Try to understand basic things about our idea first
3. Achieve the first goal

4.   Ask how we can improve on that goal
5.   Start to work toward our next goal

This simple business concept will improve our lives drastically.

Other Business Principles We Can Employ

While selling is not always our goal, we can still use the basic business concepts behind selling to improve other opportunities in our life.

First is feedback. Asking people for their feedback or input is always going to help you see the project as something more than you may have realized. You may see the opportunity develop into something more, such as a poem into a song or a short story into a novel, based on some questions from feedback.

Second, we can look at sample groups; where applicable, we can show our target audience something we are working on. This allows for an extension of the aforementioned feedback as well as gives us a chance to see genuine reactions to it. This is especially useful in public forums. Admittedly, this is more suited to artistic pursuits, but it is a useful tip all the same.

The third and final business trick we can try is one that may not seem obvious at all and is less aimed at the creative aspects, and that is looking at who your competition is. Now, for example, while you are working on your fitness, you may not want to compare directly with professional athletes, but reading interviews and books by people in the disciplines you are interested in can inspire the right attitudes toward the end goal.

Starting a Project on the Right Number

When a company is launched or a product is released on a 5 or 9 date, those numbers influence the company or product. Many numerologists pick their bank, mortgage provider, or the stores they use based on the energy that they have within their base numbers.

It can also be a good idea to consider a name for your project or product that leans into the right number energy for you. If you are doing a project about the humanitarian aspects of life, it might be a good idea to lean into a name or base number that accentuates that belief.

Releasing a product on the 5th, 9th, 14th, 18th, 23rd, or 27th of the month, with the name carefully considered, is a great idea, but so is starting the project at the right time. If your project has no end product, then instead of having a broad finish line, starting the project on these dates or dates that vibrate with your energy can have excellent results.

It is also worth keeping the movements of the celestial bodies that rule your energies in mind. If there is a retrograde effect in play, the project may need to wait until the next most suitable window of opportunity.

Even where you start a project can influence how it unfolds. Did you know that some buildings don't have a 13th floor and some apartment complexes don't have a number 13? There are even some streets that have larger numbers that skip the number 666, with the obvious connotations relating to the profane.

On the flip side of this, a great many cultures place a divinity on different numbers. It could be useful to keep this in mind, especially if that number and the energies it vibrates are complimenting you or your project.

Having one eye on the date and implementing positive aspects from cultures around us, such as sacred numbers, can help us to produce the right kinds of energy. When paired with the right name and launch date, you will most likely end up with the right outcome.

Dates and Us

We place powers on dates, anniversaries, and birthdays. These mean something to us; they hold a nostalgic pleasure in their presentation, and we afford them the time to be celebrated.

We don't do this often enough, though. When we have a project or opportunity unfolding, we don't always take the time to celebrate the small victories. Reminding yourself that you have only been working on something for a week or a month can ease the pressure you place on yourself.

Having micro celebrations can also lead to us generating positive vibrations for the various stages of our project and personal growth, making the process feel much easier than it otherwise might.

Another interesting date of consideration is February 29, which only happens every four years. It serves as the perfect kick-off date since it is unique. While it has the energy of the number 2, marking your progress solely against February 29 will mean you can look back at your journey every four years.

Thus, allowing yourself to take time off when the need dictates and when you need it will help you see how far you have come.

What Have We Learned?

We have had a look at some of the practices many large corporations use when placing products as well as the numbers taken into consideration when launching a business or product.

We have considered client and customer feedback and how we can begin to apply this to our work to better improve not only our results but also the feeling in our souls.

We have considered naming conventions and the ways we can begin to influence the energy of our projects to try and promote a much more positive outcome. We have looked at the value of a house name and touched on the value of certain numbers in culture.

We have considered the right dates on which to capitalize on the energies that vibrate the right way with our own. We have considered our relationships with dates, how we can apply the idea of micro celebrations to small victories, and how this can help us to develop our ideas and ourselves.

We can now begin to see how to apply all of the knowledge from each step of our journey and examples of how these lessons already apply in the world.

The End of Chapter Deep Dive

For this deep dive, I have two things to discuss, one that is situational but fun, and one that is a little bit bigger.

In fact, it is one of the biggest, best, and most well-known examples of numbers in our society. It has stood the test of time, and we still see it in our everyday lives.

The first example is Roman numerals. I is 1, IV is 4, and V is 5 in this system. We see them on clocks and watches and also TV and film where the copyright is normally displayed in these numerals. MMIV would be 2004, for example. We see this frequently, especially in this digital age where the end of most TV shows will display this information.

The other is Morse code, which is a rhythmic series of dots and dashes expressed in sound that translates to letters and, therefore, messages. Rhythmic sound is based on vibrations that send messages.

Both of these examples are great for us to discuss since they prove that we have long known about the relationship between words and numbers and that it is only in our increasingly skeptical age that we have begun to turn our backs on these messages.

Interestingly, the braille alphabet is a series of dots arranged in a pattern with a number attributed to each character. This is done because of the limitations of the bumps themselves, making it another example of the connection between letters and numbers.

The game series Pokemon used braille or, more accurately, a digital picture variant of braille as an in-game code for players to translate to solve puzzles.

This is just another example of language, patterns, and numbers going hand in hand in our everyday world.

Chapter 9:

Pay It Forward

There's an adage I want to discuss. Misery loves company. It means that misery seeks out more misery. There's a variation of this that you may or may not have heard. Writing begets more writing, which is to say that the act of doing something creates the opportunity to do the same thing again moving forward.

The reason this is important is that by learning what you have about the power of numbers, their effectiveness, and how best to capitalize on them, you may have begun to see the true nature of the world. However, not everyone is on the same journey.

You may, with this newfound knowledge, decide to pursue new, more challenging things. Success breeding success, encouraging others will allow you to grow, helping you to better grasp the energy that makes you who you are.

Here, we will discuss how you can and should help others on their journeys by paying the good vibrations forward.

We also have to temper this, though, because not all people are on the same stage of their journey, and many will want to come to their realizations themselves. We must learn to provide a positive vibration as best as we can without creating a negative backlash, and this can be a tricky balance to strike, especially for people who are perhaps in a difficult stage of their lives. Often, when we are in a rut, we do not always want to see the way out, so being able to communicate positivity without being pushy is an important skill.

Expressing Energy

Did you know that yawning is contagious? You may have yawned reading this, and I apologize for the use of that adage, but it is true and relevant to our conversation. Laughter is also contagious, and many a personal conversation has broken down in uproarious laughter with neither party able to recall why. This is loosely what we are discussing here.

Laughter and fatigue are energies just as much as happiness or sadness. Just like these latter two energies, we have to learn how to express them or how to make them infectious.

To express energy is to share it in motion, in speech, in action, and in feeling. It is to allow others to absorb some of your positivity by sharing a joke, a photo, or a kind word. It is something some of us already do, like sharing a holiday photo or a funny anecdote or waiting for a loved one before making the good news public.

Positive energy can be expressed in several ways. This includes talking to individuals about positive things, small acts of kindness, sharing a good book or a bag of sweets, bringing cookies to the office, or sending someone a cute puppy picture. These small acts of kindness can lead to helping people feel better, but to draw their energy to the surface, a little more needs to be done.

One of the ways to help others express themselves is to draw parallels. Use things that they might like as a basis for comparison. Consider video games. You could compare the situation you are discussing to a difficult game.

"This week's report is our big boss battle!"

This show of interest will help others feel more comfortable, allowing them to more accurately express themselves emotionally and physically. It also makes it clear that conversations between you are embarrassment-free, which will help to no end.

This is doubly important if you or the individual can be quite introverted. Even introverted people have passions, and passion can bring out the best in everyone when handled respectfully.

This is also much easier when we take into account where our energies are in relation to our ruling planets. This allows us to best capitalize on the most pronounced version of our inner energy.

If, for example, your name and personality energies align with Mercury, and Mercury is not in retrograde, you can take this as a celestial sign that the time to act is now. Whereas if Mercury is in retrograde, you may be receiving signs to wait or feelings of uncertainty or unidentified stress.

Express Yourself

One of the most important ways you can positively express energy is to express yourself honestly. Dress comfortably, talk without fear of seeming 'weird'—embracing all of the small parts of yourself is the number one way to show people what positivity can do for the soul.

Discuss the music you like, the games you've played, or the movies you've watched. If you are a little introverted, put all of these thoughts out into the world via social media. You'll soon come to see that you are not a strange person, and this opening up of the self will only encourage those around you to do the same.

Even if it is wearing something you think is too brightly colored or too black, being the best expression of yourself is key for all the happiness you will ever need.

Once people see you for who you are, many of the like-minded people will be drawn to you, becoming more relaxed to freely express themselves.

Sure, the opposite will also be true, but even the people who are opposites to you in energy will grow to respect your honesty and sincerity.

Helping Others to See Numbers

One of the trickiest parts of our journey is to show others, especially skeptics, how they too can learn to embrace the numbers. The best method is often to show where a number exists and show that this is something we already accept as part of our cosmic design, for example, with numbers like our bus routes or PINs.

Helping others to see some of the multitudes of the influential numbers in our lives can enrich their experience, even if it is only a passing understanding.

If skeptical people aren't prepared to ask questions, they may be stuck in their ideas, and we know from our experience that this could stem from their personality numbers.

But there are a great many people who are reasonably open to new ideas. Perhaps you could share both a numeroscope and a horoscope with someone, some interesting parallels, or a few contradictions.

The other thing to always keep in mind when discussing something with someone else is to be okay with them not believing in that particular thing. One of the pitfalls we as a society have is to become defensive over the things which we are passionate about or believe in. This kind of thinking only has negative connotations and only creates toxic energy. An attitude of "live and let live" is the most beneficial one we could have.

Helping Others Help Themselves

One of the ways we can help others is to tell them about our journey, about the baggage and scars we once held or that dream that at one time was unfulfilled. Even if you do not convince them to give this new way of thinking a try, sharing joy is a great sensation.

Once you have shown people that there is a positive outcome that can come from the negative they may be experiencing, they can channel that into their positive drive.

The easiest way to help others see that they can get to a better place is to show them that you have been on that same journey.

Pay It Forward

There is a simple lesson I'd like to give you now as our journey nears its end. Kindness begets kindness.

The truth is that we have to be the change we want to see in the world by understanding and embracing all we are. Only by truly embracing and nourishing all of the parts of ourselves can we begin to love ourselves. Only then we can begin to learn to share those lessons with others, to share those thoughts and successes.

We can make others part of our transformation by allowing them to share and revel in our success along with us. This will help them to feel better and perhaps encourage them to begin their journey of self-discovery and self-realization.

When we put positive energy into the ether, it comes back to us. All things, like the Earth around the Sun, are cyclical, and a circle is just another number, like the Earth's orbit, which is just another journey in numbers.

It is also worth noting that not all of the content in this book applies to only those who believe in numerology. There are a great many ideas in this journey of ours that can apply to individuals who don't believe.

Returning to our cluttered garage, we can discuss that idea in free conversation without discussing the concepts and beliefs of numerology and still be sharing the positive outcomes of our growth with someone else.

Even if someone is skeptical of feng shui or numerology, most people will agree that the idea of moving is probably the most stressful time, so discussing ideas around preparation and execution, as well as decluttering, can be the small kindness we pay forward.

And you know the funny thing about being kind to others? It will almost always lead to them being kind to you, and isn't that the point?

Enjoy the Journey

One thing I wanted to add here is a point that we can help others to understand and one that I believe is important to the happiness of the mind and soul. It is a concept that we all need to learn.

Enjoy the journey.

So often in this life, we are traveling at a thousand miles an hour, constantly moving with our heads down working hard. While that is unavoidable, there is an element of the journey passing us by.

I, of course, mean this in both the literal and metaphysical sense. All of the positivity in the world can be garnered, but it will erode quickly if we don't enjoy the moments, the plays, the musicals, the movies, the books, the songs, and anything else that makes us smile.

Companions and hobbies, entertainment and distractions—all of these things are things we need to enjoy as fervently as we can, from the taste of coffee to the smell of freshly cut grass.

Take the time to enjoy the view, even if it is on a rainy day because that moment is yours to enjoy. And how best to capitalize on our energy than to savor our journeys.

Listen to the gentle pitter-patter of the rain upon the glass window or the roof of your car. Listen to the birds singing in the morning while you sip your cup of coffee in your pajamas and just enjoy it.

We live in a beautiful, diverse world with more potential in ourselves than we can imagine. It is a world of auroras and roses, a world of music and dance and love and passion, and in all of these amazing journeys, we are one and can come to these grand vistas of chance and choice.

So, the next time you are on a train or a plane, look out the window. The next time you are in an office working or standing at a bus stop, look around and savor the smells and sounds and sights of your moment.

The next time you are with a loved one, enjoy the moment, reminisce, plan, laugh, drink tea or coffee, eat a cookie. We as people do far too little to enjoy all of these individual moments and make more.

It is so typical of us as people to concentrate on the destination and not the journey there.

What Have We Learned?

We have come a long way on our journey, and this chapter was about our energy and the effect we have on those around us by sharing our positivity and kindness and helping others begin to see the numbers in their lives. We have discussed how to pay these gifts forward, and now, we can finally put it all together.

Matching our energies with the cosmos and giving back to that same energy will begin to enrich our souls. Our journey started with the question, what is numerology? The truth is that it is everything and everywhere; it is the hidden meanings in how someone makes you feel. It is the peaceful moments of clarity, the chaos you must learn to curtail, that joy and sadness and power in you.

We looked at the power of the day we are born over our lives and the year that corresponds with us and how these things inform our needs.

We looked at the power in our names and the things we can garner from them. We even discussed how changing a name can lead to a new energy, to a new power.

We learned how to control and rebalance our chaos and how to begin to make plans to benefit our energies.

We have discussed the value of the journey, instead of our final destination, that we so often forget to savor. We looked at all of these things that have fallen before us and all of the things that we have come to understand and discuss on our journey.

And that journey, like all journeys before it and after it, all leads us to one last place.

Conclusion

Dear reader, as they say, all good things must come to an end. So, here, we will summarize what we have learned and end our journey together. It has been a long path with many laughs and some deep introspection. We have covered a lot of ground, and we have come to understand ourselves better than when we started.

We have learned about personality numbers, the power of names, and the value of using a variation of a name or using a stage name to better influence our energies.

We have looked at how we can make the numbers work for us, how we can embrace them, and how we can declutter our inner and physical space to better maintain our balance and to better control our inner chaos.

We have discussed the importance of paying forward the positivity we have in our souls and the good vibrations we command, learning how they can be brought back to us.

We have learned so much. We have talked about all of these ideas from the effect of numbers on our journeys in our day-to-day lives and their practical and accepted uses in the everyday world.

We have discussed our ancient ancestors and their apparent understanding of complex math and how they applied it to build places of power. We have discussed the relationship between the celestial bodies and their capacity to affect us.

But here we stand at the end of our journey. You'll have noticed that the previous chapter did not have an end of chapter deep dive. I wanted to make this whole section that final deep dive, that final look at a number that occurs for us all, a number we have touched on but not discussed.

This is despite it being one of the single most common numbers we will ever discuss while being a concept we determined.

What is this number?

Time.

Time is a number. It is how we measure the days, the cycles of the Moon, Earth, and stars. It is how we measure star signs and our age. It is how we measure our working week and our time off; it is how we determine deadlines and how we think of journeys.

Did you know that if every month had 28 days, there would be 13 months? I often wonder why we have 12 months rather than 13. I wonder if it is to do with the lunar cycle or the seasons.

I also wonder if the number 13, seen often as an ill omen, would be a bad sign for an entire month? I suppose we will never know, so for now, there are 365 days in a year, 52 weeks in a year, 7 days in a week, 24 hours in a day, and 60 minutes in an hour, which works out to 525,600 minutes in a year.

As you can see, time and numbers go hand in hand. We cannot be without them.

Unfortunately, much like the Sun will set, our time together has almost come to an end.

I truly hope you take the lessons we have learned, the ideas of numerology, to better reach your goals. I hope that one day this journey we have taken together can help us to begin to thrive in a world that is often so harsh.

I hope that you have taken something from this experience that helps you define who you are and rediscover the motivation you may have lost. I hope that you have found the inspiration to pursue any dreams you have.

As I said when we started this journey, I wanted to leave you with one last question and one final answer. The question is the question we started with. What is numerology?

And the answer? The answer is everything we have discussed. It is the power in our name, in our date of birth. It is the planets and stars above and the feelings and emotions within. It is the energy that guides us and the truth that sets us free.

It is a clear blue sky and a new chapter in our story. It is potential, and it is a dream realized.

It is our purpose and our hopes, the truth, and the design. It is the energy in our souls and the sky, and it is the compass that can guide us on whatever journey we embark on next.

References

Amber, M. (2016). *Person Standing Near Brown Welcome on Board-printed Floor Map*. Pexels. https://www.pexels.com/photo/jetty-feet-sign-wooden-128299/

Cottonbro (2020). *Woman Sitting on Sand*. Pexels. https://www.pexels.com/photo/woman-sitting-on-sand-4431090/

Ehlers, M. (2018a). *Assorted-color Alphabet*. Pexels. https://www.pexels.com/photo/abc-abstract-alphabet-art-1337385/

Ehlers, M. (2018b). *Red Background With 123456789 Text Overlay*. Pexels. https://www.pexels.com/photo/red-background-with-123456789-text-overlay-1329296/

Nenad, R. (2018). *Silhouette of man throw paper plane*. Pexels. https://www.pexels.com/photo/silhouette-photo-of-man-throw-paper-plane-1262304/

Numbers On Monitor. (2017). Pexels. *https://www.pexels.com/photo/airport-bank-board-business-534216/*.

Numerology Toolbox. (n.d.). *Chaldean Numerology - A deeper understanding - The numbers*. Numerology Toolbox. https://numerologytoolbox.com/numerology/chaldean-numerology/

Person About to Catch Four Dices. (2015). Pexels. https://www.pexels.com/photo/person-about-to-catch-four-dices-1111597/

Pexels (2016). *Close Up Photography of Wooden Blocks With Smile Text.* Pexels. https://www.pexels.com/photo/alphabet-blur-board-game-business-264176/

SevenStorm (2017). *123 Let's Go Imaginary Text.* Pexels. https://www.pexels.com/photo/123-let-s-go-imaginary-text-704767/

Skitterphoto (2018). *Multicolored Abacus Photography.* Pexels. https://www.pexels.com/photo/multicolored-abacus-photography-1019470/

Vibrational Science and Cosmic Creations by Meniyka Kiravell. (n.d.). *Vibrational Science Presents: A Guide to Numerology.* Kira Vell. https://kiravell.com/knowledge-is-power/a-chaldean-numerology-guide/

What Numerology Number Are You. (n.d.). *Chaldean Numerology.* Numerology Number. http://www.numerologynumber.net/types-of-numerology/chaldean-numerology#:~:text=In%20the%20Chaldean%20Numerology%20system

Wikipedia. (2020a). *Binary number.* Wikipedia. https://en.wikipedia.org/wiki/Binary_number#:~:text=In%20mathematics%20and%20digital%20electronics

Wikipedia. (2020b). *Dirac large numbers hypothesis.* Wikipedia. https://en.wikipedia.org/wiki/Dirac_large_numbers_hypothesis

Wikipedia. (2020c). *Numerology*. Wikipedia. https://en.wikipedia.org/wiki/Numerology#Chaldean_system

Wikipedia. (2020d). *Numerology*. Wikipedia. https://en.wikipedia.org/wiki/Numerology#:~:text=Pythagor as%2C%20the%20Greek%20mathematician%20and

Wikipedia Contributors (2018). *Barack Obama*. Wikipedia. https://en.wikipedia.org/wiki/Barack_Obama

Wikipedia Contributors (2019a). *Bill Gates*. Wikipedia.https://en.wikipedia.org/wiki/Bill_Gates

Wikipedia Contributors (2019b). *Dan Castellaneta*. Wikipedia. https://en.wikipedia.org/wiki/Dan_Castellaneta

Wikipedia Contributors (2019c). *Dan Reynolds (singer)*. Wikipedia. https://en.wikipedia.org/wiki/Dan_Reynolds_(singer)

Wikipedia Contributors (2019d). *David Bowie*. Wikipedia. https://en.wikipedia.org/wiki/David_Bowi

Wikipedia Contributors (2019e). *Harry Potter (character)*. Wikipedia. https://en.wikipedia.org/wiki/Harry_Potter_(character)

Wikipedia Contributors (2019f). *KT Tunstall*. Wikipedia. https://en.wikipedia.org/wiki/KT_Tunstall

Wikipedia Contributors (2019g). *Lady Gaga*. Wikipedia. https://en.wikipedia.org/wiki/Lady_Gaga

Wikipedia Contributors (2019h). *Oprah Winfrey*. Wikipedia. https://en.wikipedia.org/wiki/Oprah_Winfrey

Wikipedia Contributors (2019i). *Superman*. Wikipedia. https://en.wikipedia.org/wiki/Superman

www.ingramcontent.com/pod-product-compliance
Lightning Source LLC
Chambersburg PA
CBHW061536050726
47593CB00002B/809